Woman

WONDERFULLY MADE

Woman

WONDERFULLY MADE

Understanding Your Self-Worth and Purpose According to God

Ayesha LaNique Harris Glover

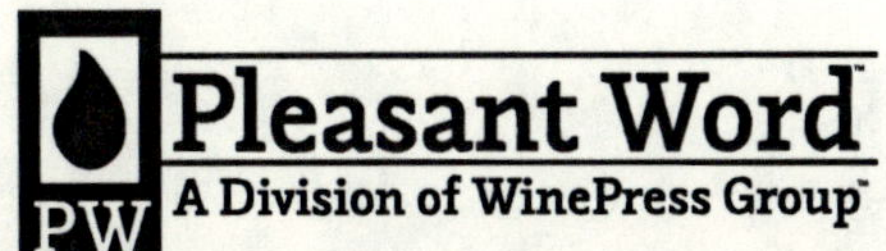

Photograph of author taken by Bob Morgan of Las Vegas, Nevada.

Foreword written by Emma Causey, Women's Ministry Leader in the Los Angeles Church of Christ.

Pleasant Word (a division of WinePress Publishing, PO Box 428, Enumclaw, WA 98022) functions only as book publisher. As such, the ultimate design, content, editorial accuracy, and views expressed or implied in this work are those of the author.

ISBN 13: 978-1-4141-1282-4
ISBN 10: 1-4141-1282-3
Library of Congress Catalog Card Number: 2008906991

Contents

Acknowledgments

This is my first book, so you know I have to thank everyone.

Thank you to Alyssa Stiff. Without your boldness in sharing your faith, life, and love for God I would not have come to recognize God as my Father.

Thank you to Sheryl Atlas. You are my "bestest" friend in the whole wide world. Your faith, sacrifice, and complete love for God have inspired me on more occasions than I could ever recall.

Thank you to Tanya Counts, my Women's Ministry Leader who is also my friend. Thank you for your guidance and helping me to mature as a Christian. Your seal of approval gave me additional confidence as a Christian writer.

Thank you to Emma Causey. Your enthusiasm and immediate response to writing the Foreword to *Woman: Wonderfully Made* was extremely encouraging to me. I am humbled and grateful for your desire to help me be successful in honoring the Lord with this book. Your support and Kingdom experience lend to my credibility as a woman of God and Christian author.

Thank you to Anne Silipo. You were the first woman in leadership in God's church that I saw in action. Your example is the picture of "a gentle and quiet spirit" (1 Peter 3:4), that God calls us, as women, to be. Only now, as a more mature Christian, do I fully appreciate gentleness and submission.

Thank you to my friend, Michelle Stainbrook. Your life situations have challenged you, yet you continue to persevere. I hope this book will encourage your heart, inspire you to embrace God in a new way, and allow you to love yourself the way God has always loved you, loves you today, and will love you eternally.

Thank you to my Sisters in the Greater Las Vegas Church of Christ and the hundreds of women I have met over the years. Your challenges, successes, and examples have inspired me to write and increased my faith in the Lord.

Thank you to Halima Todd. Your original artwork for the Wonderfully Made logo and book cover aided in the final glorious designs.

Thank you to Kerry Dean. Your editing comments and suggestions provided valuable insight that confirmed the timeliness and relevance of this message. I look forward to growing our new found friendship and I appreciate the connection *Woman: Wonderfully Made* has formed between us.

Thank you to my mama, Jacqueline Harris. You always love me like Jesus: unconditionally, sacrificially, and wholeheartedly, even when I act ugly.

Thank you to my father, Alton W. Harris. Your example taught me that I am important as a person and helped me to find my voice at a young age. You have unknowingly taught me to never take "No" for an answer.

I pray this message encourages my daughters, Ajya and Jhaelyn, to accept their eternal birthright, not as a Glover, but as a daughter to the one and only King, the Lord God Almighty. I pray you will embrace your divinity and all the Lord has in store for you in relation to your lives, hearts, spirits, relationships, bodies, work, and service to him and others.

Thank you to the love of my life, my husband, Darryl. You have never stopped holding my hand or encouraging my heart in my journey to achieve everything on my life's To Do list. No words could ever express my gratefulness and love for you and all you do for me.

Thank you to my Lord and Savior. You have rescued me from the slimy pit and have brought me to know the truth and treasure your principles. I will never be able to express my complete gratitude for your love, forgiveness and hope. I know all things are possible with you and you work for the good of those who love you. May I always find solace in you.

Foreword

The Bible has always been a source of encouragement, support, and inspiration for women. The Bible is a *divine* guide for women of noble purpose. The Bible speaks to the heart of a woman, giving her faith to live a more fruitful life. I am convinced that women have a special place in God's heart. When a woman finds God, she will discover the beauty of her life.

Ayesha has found the beauty of her life, and she shares her faith in God with creativity within the pages of *Woman: Wonderfully Made*. Scriptures are detailed throughout the reading and illuminate her resolve to be faithful as a daughter of The King.

There are special interest stories of women of the Bible whose acts of faith are worthy of imitation. Ayesha is a bright student of the truth and humbly learns from women around her on how to live by faith and not by sight; she shares some of their stories in this book, referring to them as *Divine Princesses*. Ayesha opens up about her own strengths and weaknesses, allowing you to see the person and not simply the author with a pen.

Ayesha is a great friend to many in Las Vegas (and in the Kingdom of God); knowing Ayesha is one of the greatest privileges and joys of my life. Her life in Christ is refreshing and an upward call to me and other women here in Los Angeles.

You will find yourself wanting to answer each post chapter question and picking up the book to read it again, because of your growing desire to deepen your personal convictions in the Lord. As you read *Woman: Wonderfully Made*, you will have reached into the heart of a woman who loves deeply and believes inexplicably in her calling…and your calling to live as you were designed to be—a *"Divine Princess"*.

—Emma Causey, MA, MFT
Women's Ministry Leader
Los Angeles Church of Christ

Introduction

W*oman: Wonderfully Made* speaks directly to every woman who is questioning her self-worth, is seeking to understand God better, or is confused about her place in the world. If you are uncertain of your worth and doubting why God loves you, this message will inspire you and provide you with ways to strengthen and mature your relationship with the Father. This book will help you understand how much God truly loves and adores you and wants you to believe in yourself, your birthright, position, heritage, talents, and duty as a daughter to The King.

As a woman of God, I have not always embraced the truth of being *wonderfully made*. In fact, because of my self-doubt, I took several years to write this book. I was afraid no one would want to read it, let alone buy it. I feared people who knew about my past would question my credibility as a Christian author or *Divine Princess*. I feared I would misrepresent God and somehow make him look bad. I had many fears, and Satan used them against me.

After three years I made the decision to finish the book. I decided that what people thought was not my primary concern, and that a true woman of God focuses first on what God thinks and how to please him.

The Lord has put this message on my heart for a long time. And through the years the message has evolved into this book. I now believe I would be doing God a disservice by not sharing this message with you.

In a few places in the book I call you Sister, because I wholeheartedly want to embrace you as my Sister. So no matter your race, age, experience, lifestyle, faith, beliefs, values, or biological ties, we are connected as human beings and as women. By design, this book reads like a personal conversation between you and me. I want to connect with you as if we have known each other for years.

My regular profession is as a corporate trainer. I have a Master's Degree in Educational Leadership. Therefore, I understand the principles of *active training*, one of which is that people learn best by doing, and more importantly, if you want to master something, teach it to others. *Woman: Wonderfully Made* is also my effort to master being a great daughter to the Father, The King.

In no way, shape, or form do I feel I have *arrived* at being a great daughter. Yet God has blessed me with a healthy and positive self-esteem, which has allowed me to pursue and enjoy many extraordinary experiences. And although I have fear, sadness, struggles, and sin, I diligently work to not let those things hold me back from pursuing that which I am certain is good, right, loving, and healthy.

The message I share with you through *Woman: Wonderfully Made* is one that helps you understand how valuable you are to the Lord. Believing in your value will change your life and help you pursue those things that honor the Lord and bring you forgiveness, salvation, much joy, peace, prosperity, hope, and true love.

My hope is that you will realize the fullness of your worth and birthright as a daughter to The King and begin to live your life with purpose: seeking the Lord wholeheartedly, embracing his love and promises, and using your talents to share his love with others.

Open your mind and heart and envision yourself living the concepts shared in each chapter. With each page you read, remember you are the Lord's masterpiece, he is always right, and the magnitude of his love covers all sins and *endures forever*.

Opening Prayer

Dear Father,

You are the most famous Designer ever! You have made woman to be loved, honored, beautiful, and abounding with gifts and talents. Your works are wonderful, I know that full well. Thank you for this opportunity to affect the heart of one of my Sisters. I am grateful for each word in this book and I pray you allow *Woman: Wonderfully Made* to be used for your glory. Thank you for putting this message on my heart. Thank you for creating an avenue for me to share your love and purpose with women all over the world.

Please bless my Sister who has been chosen to hear your Word through this book. In Romans 10:17, you say "faith comes from hearing the Word." So please use this message to build her faith, soften her heart, and create in her a deep and passionate longing for you that stirs her to action, seeking you with everything she has. Please help her to examine her heart as she reads each scripture and each page. Please use the questions after each chapter to develop her Christ-like character and draw her closer to you. Lord, remove every obstacle from her path and protect her against Satan's attempts to sidetrack her and dissuade her from following you. I ask that you watch over her and keep her optimistic, safe, and healthy during her spiritual journey.

Thank you for using me to help my Sister build a deeper, more meaningful relationship with you. Please place this book in the hands of thousands, even millions of women around the globe. Please allow our collective prayers to bring many women home to you surrounded by your unconditional love, constant forgiveness, eternal salvation, immeasurable hope, and perfect peace. Please answer my prayer for this message as your Daughter, your *Divine Princess*; not my will, but may your will be done.

I pray all of these things in Jesus' name,

Amen

CHAPTER 1

Designer Made

I praise you because I am fearfully and wonderfully made; your works are wonderful, I know that full well.

(Ps. 139:14)

Women love things that are designer made, whether it's a Coach purse, Jimmy Choo shoes, a Vera Wang dress, or even diamond jewelry designed by the late Harry Winston. We love designer things. We will do more, work harder, beg, borrow, and steal for authentic goods. Well, I'm here to tell you, Sister, you are Designer Made. And not by any old designer, but created by the best and most innovative and talented designer of all—God, the Creator of the Universe.

When I think about the creation of woman, I get goose bumps. I love knowing the Creator of the Universe, who created all things, created you…and me.

You are like no other. You have been intricately designed. You are unique and special in the eyes of God. There has never been and never will be another *you*!

When God created the universe, he used his artistic, loving, and omnipotent mind to speak into being the planets, stars, oceans, animals, trees, and plants. He waited until the right moment to create man. Five days he spent creating all the things that he knew would bring peace and joy to your heart and provide you with the sustenance necessary for you to live, not just survive, but to live in abundance.

The first chapter of Genesis explains that on the sixth day God created man in his image. God purposefully placed man in charge of all living things because man was designed to be superior to everything else on the Earth (Ps. 8:6-8). The Lord spent time looking for a companion that was perfect for the man he had created. When he found none among all the other animals, God made you…woman. Woman was the final piece of artwork God formed—the finishing touch that brings all else together.

You were not an afterthought, but the final *masterpiece* to the formation of the universe. With *you* his majestic creation was *complete!*

Wow! Doesn't that make you feel special? I am inspired every day knowing the Lord put time and specific thought into creating me…woman.

Woman is not just a pretty sidekick to man. Woman plays one of the most essential and intricate roles in history; every day honored for her love, courage, service, and example, and forever remembered in women like Mary, Esther, and Deborah.

Sadly, many women have forgotten or never realized who they are. They place their self-esteem in the hands of sinful and flawed people who have distorted views of humanity. Then women fail to accept their positions as daughters of The King, thereby failing to realize their rights as daughters, their God-given talents, and their responsibilities as *a woman*.

So many women hate themselves. They hate how they look. They think they have no talents or skills. I have heard many women say, "I could never do that." "I'm not smart enough." Or, "I'm not pretty enough." I have said those things.

As women, we often fail to recognize our talents and we never seem to be satisfied with our bodies and the way we look. We allow society and its twisted thinking to tell us what is beautiful. And when we don't match up to the perfect look of the month we feel ugly, stupid, and hopeless. That has *got* to end!

The Lord tells you that you are "fearfully and wonderfully made" (Ps. 139:14). What does that mean? It means you were created to be awed and revered as a holy, powerful, gifted, and beautiful masterpiece of the Lord. Human beings are the Lord's *magnum opus*: his single greatest work. Nothing in all creation is greater than you!

When I reflect upon my own creation, I am reminded of Psalm 139:13, “For you created my inmost being; you knit me together in my mother’s womb.” With his own hands the Lord created me. He designed my nose, lips, hips, and thighs. The size 11 shoe I wear is part of his design. He gave me my personality: bold, passionate, motivated, and creative. And yet, at times, I have struggled to love *how* God created me. I have wished and prayed for green eyes, bigger breasts, smaller hips, longer hair, and so on. Those things are not eternal. Nor will they bring me eternal happiness. My joy, my confidence must come from God, not a 36”-24”-36” figure. I am beautiful to my Father. And better yet, I will be beautiful *and* flawless in heaven. And until I get there, God is not judging me by my cup size or the size of my hips. He loves me no matter what. He loves me in ways I cannot imagine. God, *my* Father, loves me even when I do not love myself.

Your true self-esteem and self-worth have to come from God. He created you. He knows his creation is good, and God is never wrong!

As you accept your position as a daughter of The King, you become spiritual royalty. You become a princess—a *Divine Princess*, in fact.

As a divine being, please don’t be confused with being a god or being God. Rather, as a *divine* being you are of God and God-like because the ability to display God’s character was placed in your heart when you were made in his image. Nothing else God created was made in his image—only mankind, only you. You have the power within you to display the character of God, the Father of the universe. This power is mysterious, though. It doesn’t work simply because you want it to. This power that I am referring to comes to life and takes shape when you receive God as your Father and give your heart back to him. God gave you your heart first, literally and figuratively. As you grow and mature you must give your heart back to the Lord in order to receive your spiritual inheritance as a child of God. Then, you can achieve your full, God-given traits and potential. Without this transfer of heart, you can never experience all of the divine blessings, gifts, grace and mercy the Father has in store for you.

Being divine is not about being perfect, whether in your looks, thoughts, behavior, or character. Being a princess is not about palaces, financial wealth, or being waited on hand and foot. Therefore, being a *Divine Princess* is a spiritual concept, where worldly definitions take a back seat to spiritual definitions. My goal is to make this concept clear to you, so that you will understand your self-worth is defined by God. It is a certainty that God loves you completely without pretense or conditions. The Father's desire is for you to take your place in his family, love yourself the way he loves you, and share his eternal and unconditional love with others.

The Lord wants you to see your reflection in the mirror and feel beautiful, not just because of the way you look, but rather because of the love in your heart, how you share that love with others, and your continual devotion to him.

I could tell you lies like Satan does about monetary wealth, outward beauty, and worldly fame, but I would be doing the Lord, you, and myself a great disservice. Is your nose the right shape? Maybe not according to the most prestigious plastic surgeon, a sinner and flawed man himself. Yet, it is according to God! Is your hair the right color? Maybe not according to the latest fashion magazine, created and operated by the opinions of narrow-minded and imperfect people. Yet, it is according to God.

If you decide to change your appearance in some way, first ask yourself, why you want to do that. Please pray about your situation, if your answer includes things like:

- I will finally like myself;
- Others will like me;
- I'll be more accepted by other people;
- I will obtain the desires of my heart;
- This change will please so and so;
- I won't be depressed any more;
- My relationship with my boyfriend or husband will improve; and etc.

Seek advice from an honest and trustworthy friend, and think twice about what you are about to do.

Determine the underlying reasons for wanting to change your appearance. If they have something to do with self-loathing or fantasy outcomes, you must deal with the real issues. Neither something as small as coloring your hair nor the more extreme of plastic surgery will change those deep-seated issues that plague your heart, mind and spirit.

Sister, I'm not telling you that it's bad to color your hair, have plastic surgery done, or to somehow change or improve your appearance. What I am saying is make sure your motives are pure and healthy. God made you specifically, just as he intended, down to the last detail. He knew what he was doing. He wasn't wrong, bored, or preoccupied. All he wants you to do is appreciate and love yourself the way he loves you. The Lord does not want you to determine your worth based on magazine covers, the latest TV show, or the opinions of sinful men. He wants you to live confidently knowing you are beautiful and unique—an *original* masterpiece of the Creator of the Universe.

There are no stars in the sky that can shine brighter than you in God's eyes. There are no mysteries of the Earth that God admires more than you. He created you in his likeness. So believe this—the Father has created nothing more magnificent than you...*woman: fearfully and wonderfully made.*

DEEPEN YOUR PERSONAL CONVICTIONS

READ: Genesis 1-2; Psalm 139:13-16

1. Write out the definition of "*magnum opus*".

2. Why are you considered the Lord's "magnum opus"?

3. What one thing will you change in your thinking to believe you are the Lord's original masterpiece?

4. Pray daily for your mind and heart to fully believe that you are the Lord's masterpiece and have his love unconditionally and eternally.

CHAPTER 2

Made in His Divine Image

God created human beings; he created them godlike, reflecting God's nature. He created male and female. God blessed them. "Prosper! Reproduce! Fill Earth! Take charge!"

(Gen. 1:27-28, THE MESSAGE)

You have the ability to reflect God's nature. No one can rob you of this fact and knowledge. *Today* and every day to come, you decide to embrace the power of God in your life and to be the *Divine Princess* you were created to be. Your inherent divinity was freely placed within your heart by God.

You were made a little lower than the heavenly beings and then crowned...with glory and honor and made to rule over everything the Father has created (Ps. 8:5-8). As a reflection of God you are *divine, fearfully and wonderfully made* in his image to have the traits and characteristics of your majestic creator.

Wow! Created in God's own divine image. Until I wrote this chapter I'd never done a study on the image of God. I just took it for granted that my minister was right when he said I was made in God's image. But what does that *really* mean?

What is God's image, his nature? How does the Bible describe God?

God Is Love

> Everyone who loves has been born of God and knows God. Whoever does not love does not know God, because God is love.
>
> (1 John 4:7-8)

God has made you a loving creature. Therefore since you love, you have the ability to know God. It is a woman's passion to love well and her intense desire to *be loved* well.

Somewhere deep within you, you know how to love like no other. When a woman is truly in touch with her natural ability and gift to love, her family is drawn to her. Mama, Grandma, Sister, Best Friend, Loving Wife are all names used to call on woman. Nothing can heal a wound, great or small, like the gentle and warm kiss of Mom. Women have this godly ability to make others feel loved, supported, and secure with just a hug, a smile, or a wink.

Poems, books and songs have been written about a mother's love, the love of a good woman, and loving a woman. There is something immensely special and unique about receiving love from a woman. That something special is God. He knew you…woman, would be the one to carry his legacy of love throughout history—from the beginning with Adam and Eve, until the end of time, when Jesus returns.

God Embodies the Fruit of the Spirit

> The fruit of the Spirit is love, joy, peace, patience, kindness, goodness, faithfulness, gentleness and self-control.
>
> (Galatians 5:22-23)

God embodies all of these qualities and he bestowed them upon you when he created you in his image. You may feel like you are lacking in one or more of these areas, however, with God you lack no good thing. In fact, Scripture says God arms you with strength and makes your way perfect (Ps. 18:32).

So since God is love, you are love. As God is patient, you are patient. As God is good, you are good. As God is self-controlled, you are self-controlled. So why don't you feel or act this way? Unless you wholeheartedly seek the Lord and make Jesus Lord of your life, you will not be able to achieve love, patience, goodness, self-control or any fruit of the Spirit for a sustained period of time. God makes your way perfect, so the opposite is true, as well. Without God you are imperfect; thus your need to be close to the Lord.

Surely, even before I was a Christian I had shown love to my family and friends, been kind to strangers, even remained self-controlled in moments when I could have been unruly. So yes, without being close to God I can be nice and show love to others. However, without God my motives for being nice and loving are questionable. Did I do it because I wanted something? Something tangible like a toy, or money, or sex? Or something intangible like acceptance, recognition, or freedom?

Without God my motives, although they may seem trivial and may not hurt anyone are not pure; they are not godly. When I do things, even today, often my first instinct is what's in it for me (WIIFM). As I walk with God, and my relationship with him matures, I am compelled to examine my heart regularly. Do I do the things I do because I want something in return, or do I do them because I love God and I want to do what is righteous, not just right?

Even in writing this book, I pray for God to continue to humble my heart. To not look for the fame and prestige that comes from being a published author, rather I ask God to use the message in this book to reach the women who need to hear it and are seeking him. I pray for God to use me as a tool to get his message to women who are hurting, confused, or want to deepen their relationship with him. Yet, I like receiving praise. I don't mind being in the limelight, so my worldly "princess" mentality can easily become arrogant and boastful. My sinful nature is strong, so I cling to the Lord to guide me so my motives remain pure. I want to be like Jesus, who came to seek and save the lost (Luke 19:10), and not receive personal glory as the Son of The King.

The Lord wrote each of his qualities on your heart. Being in his presence, in his fellowship, allows you to tap into his power within you, thereby embracing your divinity and displaying the Fruit of the Spirit: love, joy, peace, patience, kindness, goodness, faithfulness, gentleness, and self-control.

The Word says God created you in his image. Surely he believes you can rise to the occasion and honor him with your life. He has confidence in you…his wonderful creation. He knows your gifts, talents, and character because he gave them to you. Your talents and fine character were his first.

When you study the creation of the universe, you can see God's character and talents.

God Is Light

Throughout the Bible, God is referred to as being the light (Ps. 27:1), having light (Ps. 4:6), giving light (Ps. 19:8; Ps. 119:130), and being resplendent with light (Ps. 76:4). Likewise people, especially women, are often referred to as radiant or glowing, like when a woman is pregnant. This is not just an indication of her outer beauty, but more a sign of her inner beauty spilling out onto everything she touches.

God tells you to "let your light shine before men" (Matt. 5:16). God knows that if you remain in him you "shine like stars in the universe as you hold out the word of life" (Phil. 2:15-16). Again, in Daniel 12:3, "[Women] who are wise will shine like the brightness of the heavens, and [women] who lead many to righteousness, like the stars for ever and ever."

The Lord created you to shine with his reverent and magnificent light visible to all; to transform the life of each person you touch with his spirit and vitality.

Remember that one of the first things God did when he created the universe was to create light (Gen. 1:3).

God Is Creative

God creates magnificent things and creatures. The design of human beings, how we look, how we think and function is amazing. I am often intrigued by how God made man and woman to "fit together" physically for the purpose of becoming one, making love, and creating children. It's unique and intimate, specifically designed to create unity and oneness between a husband and wife. In God's design, people are allowed to create another person. Now that is truly amazing.

In addition, the Lord's supreme imagination created the planets, stars, oceans, lands, animals, trees, and plants. You may be a great artist too, a dancer, singer, skilled crafts woman, or even a problem solver. Your innovation, creativity, and attention to detail are an inspiration from God.

God Is Wise

God has more knowledge than the greatest and largest Think Tank in the world. More knowledge than all the geniuses combined. He knows how everything works. Ya' know how people say, "It's not brain surgery or you don't have to be a rocket scientist to..." in reference to being smart. Well, God is the first brain surgeon, and heart surgeon, and astronaut, and rocket scientist. He is never confused. He always has the answer. Nothing gets past the Creator of the Universe. He sees all, knows all, and understands all.

In his wisdom, the Lord created the body to heal itself, perform functions without conscious thought, and house such physical and mental strength and power. He constructed your wonderful body, mind, and soul.

And what about the stars: they just hang there in the sky. How do they do that? God knows; he created the concept. He created the theories of relativity, gravity, and energy. The Creator of all shared his wisdom and intellect with you in various ways: science, mathematics, language, communication, business, arts, philosophy, athletics, technology, and spirituality.

God Is Loving

The Lord displayed his love when he didn't want Adam to be alone. He showed care and concern for Adam. God labored and spent time going through every animal until he found Adam a helpmate. When he found no suitable helpmate, the Father created Eve as the perfect mate for Adam to enjoy for a lifetime. In the same way, you love others to the point of working tirelessly, creating things you know are perfect for them. You love so much you would willingly sacrifice your life for someone you love deeply. Is that not God-like?

God Is Hospitable

The Lord created a special place for Adam and Eve—the Garden of Eden. He worked until he had met all of their needs. In fact, he took care of their basic needs of air, water, food, and shelter prior to creating them. Even after Adam and Eve were created, he continued to meet their needs and allowed them to prosper even outside of the Garden of Eden. In the same way, your hospitable nature makes sure the people in your life—family and friends, as well as strangers—have what they need to feel loved and well taken care of, and to prosper.

God Is Righteous

From the beginning the Lord has displayed his righteous nature and his desire for righteousness in his sons and daughters. When Adam and Eve disobeyed God and ate from the Tree of Knowledge, they sinned against God. As their punishment for sinning they could no longer live in God's holy garden.

A righteous heart pursues what is right and good and obeys the Lord willingly. A righteous heart is troubled by injustice and evil, and looks for opportunities to put God's principles into practice. In you, God has placed a longing for righteousness and his ability to maintain the standards of what is right and just.

God Is Patient

The very nature of God is abounding in patience. He was patient in creating the universe. He did not rush. He attended to the infinite details of the animals, landscaping, and stars.

God showed patience with Adam and Eve even after they disobeyed them. His nature was gentle, yet he was able to enforce discipline. Within your soul you possess patience. Could it be that you have shown patience with your close girlfriend long after someone else would have given up on her or become frustrated and angry with her? Deep within you, you have what God possesses and what every child needs in a parent—an endless wellspring of patience, gentleness, and security.

God Is Assertive

The Creator of the Universe spoke everything into being.

> And God said, "Let there be light," and there was light.
>
> (Gen. 1:3)

The Lord does not shy away from opportunity or approach situations with an uncertain heart. He knows what he wants and he goes after it. He wants you. This book is another way he is calling and speaking directly to you. You may be able to state clearly what you need and want, and even advocate for the young, weak, or disadvantaged by using your strong voice and talents from God.

God Is Confident

After God was done creating the universe and everything in it, he "saw all that he had made and it was very good" (Gen. 1:31). Confidence, not arrogance is a true trait of the Lord. When someone asks you what your skills are and you can immediately recognize and state your talents, that is like the Maker of the Universe. The Lord has full confidence in his skills. And he gave you confidence.

> But [you] are not of those who shrink back and are destroyed, but of those who believe and are saved.
>
> (Heb. 10:39)

God Is Able to Stop and Smell the Roses

On the seventh day the Lord rested. He saw the beauty around him and took time to bask in the glory of all he had made. Often times we are so busy that we forget to stop and smell the roses. We act like Martha, overwhelmed by the details and forget to enjoy the moment—instead of being more like Mary, who took time to appreciate the importance of what was happening right then (Luke 10:38-42). Just like God, Jesus knew when to rest, when to listen, when to fellowship, when to let things go, when to work, when to preach, when to forgive, and when to slow down to love well. If you help others to relax and appreciate life, you are a blessing to them, and your efforts are directly related to God.

God Has Strength and Endurance

The Father spent six days working to create everything. Everything! That requires a mental and physical strength beyond imagination. He persevered until he was done. Jesus endured physical, emotional, and spiritual hardship and still ran his race until the end. In the same way, the strength you possess to endure hardships and struggles was given to you by God.

The Lord knows exactly what you can handle and he gives you no more than that (1 Cor. 10:13). He is certain of your ability to withstand physical, emotional, and mental trials because you have his strength and love which endure forever.

God Has Hope

I love that the Lord never loses hope in me. He never loses hope in you. In the Garden of Eden he had hope for Adam and Eve that they would not eat from the Tree of Knowledge. He knew his warnings were in vain. He knew they would disobey, and history would unfold. However, just like any human parent, the heavenly Father maintains a hope for you. Even through your disobedience, rebellion, and hatred towards him, his hope for your salvation and eternal life in heaven remains steadfast.

If you are a mother, or have a best friend, or you have ever been in love, you know hope. You hope your child will be successful in every endeavor. You hope your best friend will receive every desire of her heart. And you hope the love you have found is your soulmate. The Lord hopes you will acknowledge him and rely upon his spirit that you were given as his holy creation: a spirit of love, joy, peace, patience, kindness, goodness, faithfulness, gentleness, and self-control.

There are many other majestic characteristics of God that he planted deep within your soul. Just know that as a woman, every good thing you are, every wonderful quality or talent you possess is a trait directly inherited from the Lord, the Creator of the Universe.

Deepen Your Personal Convictions

Read: 1 John 4:7-12; Galatians 5:22-23

1. List at least three characteristics that you have that are from God.

2. List three ways you show or use the characteristics listed above.

3. Why do you have trouble consistently displaying the godly character within you?

4. Pray daily to use the godly characteristics you have been given to honor Christ and love others.

CHAPTER 3

Designer Price Tag

For you know that it was not with perishable things such as silver or gold that you were redeemed from the empty way of life handed down to you from your forefathers, but with the precious blood of Christ, a lamb without blemish or defect.

(1 Pet. 1:18–19)

As a designer creation you came with a designer price tag. You were expensive! Paid not with mere silver or gold, or dollars, or even diamonds or rubies, you were paid for with the blood of God's only son, your Lord and Savior, Jesus Christ.

There is no price tag greater than the life of another. Ask any parent who has lost a child. As a society we generally place great value on human life. Those who have given their life to save another are called *heroes* and *martyrs*. As a parent I cannot imagine asking my daughter to lay down her life for someone else, especially knowing she would be tortured and her sacrifice would be ignored and discounted by so many people.

God sacrificed Jesus knowing there was no certainty that you would love and obey him in return or desire to be with him. Yet, because of his *divine* love for you and the memory of Jesus' sacrifice, he maintains hope that each day you will arise and place your trust in him to guide your life.

Can you imagine paying millions or billions of dollars just for the *hope* of something wonderful or powerful happening? God sacrificed Jesus *hoping* you would devote yourself to him. He knew you might not, yet he *hoped* you would.

From most of the world Jesus has not even received a simple "thank you" for his sacrifice. And even some who profess Jesus Christ as Lord and Savior lack true devotion and obedience to him and lack gratefulness for his grace and mercy (Matt. 7:21-27).

The payment of Jesus' life for yours allows you to have a relationship with the Father. Without his sacrifice and complete love and devotion to God, you would remain lost...a slave to sin…an alien...an orphan for eternity.

God loves you so much he was willing to allow his own son's horrific death just so you may live a righteous and blessed life and have a relationship with him. The Father has placed the ultimate price tag on your life (John 3:16). According to the Lord you have value far beyond the largest and most precious jewels in the world.

God loves you so much and places such value on your life that it is a disgrace to God when you do not love or value yourself. How dare you not love and cherish what the Lord has created and paid for with the ultimate sacrifice!

The Lord is saddened every time he hears you put yourself down, shrink back from your God-given talents, or lack love and respect for his divine creation, his masterpiece…*you.*

I know there have been times in my life where I have not loved myself well and I have not shown gratefulness for the Lord's sacrifice and mercy. At these times I know I have broken the Lord's heart.

Yet, more than any human parent, your heavenly Father wants you to do well, to be successful, happy, loved, healthy, and peaceful. When you do not love yourself well, he feels pain and sadness. However, God never gets so fed up with you that he discards you (like I would in my sinful nature). When I am tired of someone doing bad things over and over again, I get frustrated and don't want to have any more to do with that person.

Fortunately, God is not like that! He has patience that lasts an eternity, and love deeper than any ocean. All which he lavishes on you.

Ask yourself, would the Lord *really* ignore and disregard the very woman he let his son die for? Or would God pursue that woman until she reciprocated his feelings, making sure *the sacrifice* was ultimately worth it, and that his love would continue in her?

God would rather let Jesus die again and again and again, so that you would love him. It may sound desperate, yet actually it is a profound and often incomprehensible statement of love, sacrifice, and hope.

The Lord promises he will never leave you nor forsake you (Josh. 1:5). I know it's hard to believe the Father will never give up on you. However, the sacrifice...*the payment*...for your love was too great. Giving up would make Jesus' sacrifice seem worthless, futile, and unimportant. And it is definitely none of those things!

Deepen Your Personal Convictions

Read: Luke 23:13-49

1. How do you think God felt knowing his son was going to be tortured and sacrificed?

2. If you were God how would you want people to respond to your son's sacrifice?

3. What will you do to honor the sacrifice Jesus made for you?

4. Pray daily to live a life worthy of the sacrifice Jesus made for you.

CHAPTER 4

Spiritual Inheritance

For this reason Christ is the mediator of a new convent, that those who are called may receive the promised eternal inheritance....

(Heb. 9:15)

A spiritual inheritance, what is that comprised of? What is the daughter of The King destined to inherit? It is my pleasure to share with you the birthright of a faithful and obedient daughter of The King. As a woman, you are the recipient of God's great and powerful love. And because of Jesus' sacrifice for you, you have the privilege of becoming a child of God, free to receive the boundless gifts, blessings, promises, and riches of the Lord. Behold the abundant gifts of your spiritual inheritance.

Unconditional Love

> Who shall separate us from the love of Christ? Shall trouble or hardship or persecution or famine or nakedness or danger or sword?...No, in all these things we are more than conquerors through him who loved us. For I am convinced that neither death nor life, neither angels nor demons, neither the present nor the future, nor any powers, neither height nor depth, nor anything else in all creation, will be able to separate us from the love of God that is in Christ Jesus our Lord.
>
> (Rom. 8:35, 37-39)

You will never experience a love more freeing than the love of God. Terry McMillan's book *Waiting to Exhale* brings to life the friendship and love between four women.

My understanding of the concept of *waiting to exhale* is that in a truly loving relationship you can be yourself and the person will still love you even after they know all your flaws and sins. You are free of all your anxieties, inhibitions, and fears, and thus you can stop holding your breath in fear. You can finally breathe deeply knowing you do not have to bear your burdens alone or at all.

God loves you like this. His unconditional love surrounds you and you are free to live joyously, peacefully, and transparently because of the security found in God's unfailing love. He knows all about your talents, passions, successes, struggles, and failures. He knows about *every* sin you have ever committed. And he still loves you completely. God, the Father, will never leave you.

Powerful Mercy

> But because of his great love for us, God, who is rich in mercy, made us alive with Christ even when we were dead in transgressions—it is by grace you have been saved.
>
> (Eph. 2:4-5)

Mercy is *not receiving* what you deserve. As a sinner you deserve just punishment for your sins. You deserve the consequences of your actions every time you sin. You deserve death which is the wages of sin (Rom. 6:23).

God has not given you the punishment you deserve. Instead Jesus, who was holy and blameless before the Lord, took your place and received the guilty verdict you deserve. Jesus was brutally punished and served your sentence for you. The Father's mercy has spared you from certain death. The fact that you are reading this book is a sign of you living and breathing. Each day God's mercy affords you multiple "second chances" to powerfully change your life and embrace the *divine* woman you were created to be.

Genuine Grace

> For it is by grace you have been saved, through faith—and this not from yourselves, it is the gift of God—not by works, so that no one can boast.
>
> (Eph. 2:8-9)

Grace is receiving what you *do not* deserve. As a sinner you deserve nothing. Yet the Father has literally allowed himself to die so you can have every good thing this life and heaven has to offer. He allows you to experience love, happiness, prosperity, and many tangible gifts you take for granted because of his grace and love for you.

It is by the gift of grace that you may be saved. Without God's grace you would be lost forever. There is nothing, no work you can do to earn the Lord's grace. He simply gives it to you, because he loves you.

Selfless Sacrifices

> For God so loved the world that he gave his one and only Son, that whoever believes in him shall not perish but have eternal life.
>
> (John 3:16)

As a parent I cannot imagine giving up my child, even to save the life of another. Yet God not only gave up his only son, he then allowed him to be brutally tortured and handed over to vicious and unspiritual people to be crucified. He did all this for you because he loves you and wants to have a deep and personal relationship with you. God was willing to sacrifice his *only* son, so *you* would have the opportunity to live abundantly and eternally in heaven.

Forgiveness that Heals

> Praise the Lord, O my soul, and forget not all his benefits—who forgives all your sins and heals all your diseases; who redeems your life from the pit and crowns you with love and compassion.
>
> (Ps. 103:2-4)

All your sins forgiven, have you ever heard a more wonderful phrase? Your slate wiped clean. Does your biological family offer you that kind of forgiveness? Has your boss removed every transgression and mistake from your employee file? Do you forgive yourself the way God forgives?

Every sin washed away by the blood of Christ is a gift reserved for those who accept the Lord as their Savior, become children of God, and obey God's every command. The Father's forgiveness heals your soul. *Every* weight is lifted from your shoulders and you are free to live as a *Divine Princess*, pursuing every thing that is good, right, and godly. This absolute truth may seem incomprehensible, yet it does not detract from its realness or the peace that follows being healed.

Uplifting Salvation

> My soul finds rest in God alone; my salvation comes from him. He alone is my rock and my salvation; he is my fortress, I will never be shaken.
>
> (Ps. 62:1-2)

Your heavenly Father has provided you with a Savior; someone to rescue you from the darkness, pull you out of the slimy pit of sin, and lift you up to the light on to solid ground. As much as I love my biological father, he cannot save me. As much as I rely on my husband, he cannot save me. There is *only* one who can save you. That is Jesus Christ. The blood he shed on the cross for you he did out of love and reverence for God. He is offering you sincere, eternal, and majestic salvation. *Every* sin you have ever committed will be taken away. You can be free of your bondage of sin because of Jesus.

Divine Intercession

> Therefore he is able, once and forever, to save those who come to God through him. He lives forever to intercede with God on their behalf.
>
> (Heb. 7:25, NLT)

As Jesus died on the cross for you, and you accept him as your Lord and Savior, he is eternally committed to represent you before God. Then, everyday when you sin, Jesus steps in between you and the Father and shields you from the punishment that you deserve for sinning against God, yourself, and others. Your sins are forever washed away by the blood Christ shed on the cross. Your slate is wiped clean. The love and sacrifice of Jesus gives you the opportunity to appear before the Lord perfect and unblemished.

When I was growing up I always wished I had a big brother to look after me and protect me from the evil of this world. When I was a teenager I didn't realize the role Jesus wanted to play in my life. He has always been there to be that big brother I wanted, but I didn't recognize him as my rock, my Savior, my intercessor, until I was an adult.

Eternal Life

> The Father loves the Son and has placed everything in his hands. Whoever believes in the Son has eternal life, but whoever rejects the Son will not see life, for God's wrath remains on him.
>
> (John 3:35-36)

This world is caught up with eternal youth and living forever. Sixty is the new forty and thirty is the new twenty-one. Plastic surgeons are making a gazillion dollars as people, especially women, are literally dying to maintain a more youthful appearance.

The fountain of youth is still sought after all around the globe. The real fountain of life or, as the Bible says, "living water" (John 4:7-14) that provides immortality and stops the hands of time can only be found in Jesus. Through Jesus you can live forever in heaven where there is no pain, no worries, and no tears (Rev. 21:4).

As age conscious as the world is you'd think there would be more people *dying* to become Christians so they could *live* forever.

The Kingdom of Heaven

> Praise be to the God and Father of our Lord Jesus Christ! In his great mercy he has given us new birth into a living hope through the resurrection of Jesus Christ from the dead, and into an inheritance that can never perish, spoil or fade—kept in heaven for you.
>
> (1 Pet. 1:3–4)

Heaven is a glorious sanctuary from this life where you live eternally with the Father in peace, joy, and love. The Lord is preparing a place in heaven for every one of his daughters.

Heaven is a mystical and mysterious place. I love that about it; that fact allows me to use my big imagination to picture what heaven will be like. The Bible doesn't clearly depict heaven, making it hard to describe. Yet, many days I imagine what my room looks like in heaven. I envision all my favorite things, colors, and sounds. I imagine being able to fly in heaven, never being tired, sick, or old, and always being surrounded by love. I pray I will be able to eat anything I want to and not gain one pound! No matter what picture I may create in my mind, I am certain heaven will be far beyond everything wonderful you or I could envision.

Immeasurable Hope

> Blessed is [she] whose help is the God of Jacob, whose hope is in the Lord [her] God, the Maker of heaven and earth, the sea, and everything in them—the Lord, who remains faithful forever.
>
> (Ps. 146:5-6)

No matter what kind of day you may be having or how low you may feel at any given moment, faith in Jesus allows you to keep immeasurable hope in your heart. A woman who has hope knows the Lord "works for the good of those who love him, who have been called according to his purpose" (Rom. 8:28). Hope allows you to believe that no matter how tragic your situation, God has the power to work it out for your good.

I love knowing that no matter what struggle I may be suffering through, God is always there to help me. I have hope because I know he will see me through and with him I will overcome my situation. I rarely feel defeated and like nothing can be done. My God gives me hope in all situations: illness, death, every stage of my marriage, parenting challenges, business setbacks, income loss,… you name it and I am certain God will prevail.

Perfect Peace

> You will keep in perfect peace him whose mind is steadfast, because he trusts in you. Trust in the LORD forever, for the LORD, the LORD, is the Rock eternal.
>
> (Isa. 26:3-4)

Faith and steadfastness in the Lord bring perfect peace. In today's world there are so many things to worry about; to fill your heart with anxiety. Yet as a faithful follower of Christ you can experience a deep sense of peace even in the midst of turmoil.

You can see those around you succumbing to stress and fear, their hearts heavy and burdened with the worries of this life. You may feel like this right now. Yet a woman who rests her burdens with the Lord has a light and joyful heart. Come and find rest with the Lord. He is waiting for you right now; ready to lift those heavy burdens from your shoulders. The Father has prepared a special place just for you. He is watching the road daily, waiting for you to come home.

Complete Joy

> Until now you have not asked for anything in my name. Ask and you will receive, and your joy will be complete.
>
> (John 16:24)

I have asked the Lord for so many things over the years, both tangible and intangible things. Usually his answer is, "Yes." But often he has said, "No." I don't always understand why, and yet I know his answer is always right. I can find contentment in his response even when I wanted and prayed for something else. Ultimately my joy does not come from the Lord's answer to my prayer, but from knowing I am his daughter, whom he loves and protects, and for whom he provides all necessities for living abundantly.

For the world temporary joy comes from worldly possessions, false love, selfish desires, impure pursuits, and revenge on others. Yet for the godly, complete and lasting joy comes from walking with Christ and storing up treasures in heaven where there is no pain or sin.

> A joyful spirit is evidence of a grateful heart.
>
> (Maya Angelou)

Your joy is a direct measure of your gratefulness for his unconditional love and all the blessings the Lord has given you.

The following activity is designed to open your eyes to the simple blessings and pleasures we often take for granted. Stop the activity before you pass out or cause yourself harm.

If you are having trouble recognizing the blessings in your life, take your left hand and tightly cover your mouth, then take your thumb and index finger on your right hand and squeeze your nose. Do this for three minutes and see how grateful you are for oxygen and the inherent ability to breathe freely.

Timeless Guidance

> All Scripture is God-breathed and is useful for teaching, rebuking, correcting and training in righteousness, so that the [wo]man of God may be thoroughly equipped for every good work.
>
> (2 Tim. 3:16-17)

Your God created you to be great, not on your own, but with his timeless wisdom, always available, and consistently correct. He will never lead you in the wrong direction or give you flawed advice. His Scriptures will prepare you for every good work.

As much as I love and admire my girlfriends and spiritual advisors, they are human and can be wrong. When you turn to the Lord for guidance, rest assured you will always find wisdom that applies to your current situation. You will find clarity in the midst of confusion. You will find peace when you are harried. You will find comfort when you feel lonely. The Lord's Word will *never* lead you astray.

> [God's] word is a lamp to [your] feet and a light to [your] path.
>
> (Ps. 119:105)

A Crown of Glory

> And when the Chief Shepherd appears, you will receive the crown of glory that will never fade away.
>
> (1 Pet. 5:4)

As the Lord does with any princess, he wants to crown you with glory. Yet the glory is his glory, not your own. And this crown is received upon completing the race marked out for you. It is a crown that will never fade. It is eternal.

Imagine each jewel represents a moment when you suffered and turned to Jesus to lift you up. The gold in the crown has been tested and molded just right…to fit your head. This crown has been fashioned by the Greatest Designer as you have given yourself to him, and upon completing the race you reflect his image, his heart of perseverance, courage, love, and hope.

Even More Than You Can Imagine

> Now to him who is able to do immeasurably more than all we ask or imagine, according to his power that is at

> work within us, to him be glory in the church and in Christ Jesus throughout all generations, for ever and ever! Amen.
>
> (Eph. 3:20-21)

Now I don't know about you, but I can image a lot. My brain never stops working. Yet the Bible says God can do "immeasurably more" than you or I can imagine. What can you imagine? What images come to mind? A loving and fulfilling marriage? Healthy and successful children? A well paying job? Supportive friends and family? What?

Whatever you are envisioning, the Lord can do that and better! I am so encouraged by that. Even more important than the tangible things you can envision, God can do immeasurably more *within* you than you ever thought was possible. He can transform your heart, allowing you to forgive others who have hurt you. The Father can heal your emotional wounds. He can heal you from addictions or co-dependency. He can help you love your enemies who betray and slander you at every opportunity. He can even give you distaste for the sins in which you find yourself engaged. What God can do on the inside of you is even more exciting and powerful than what he can do on the outside.

As I write this section, in the background a song is playing by Kirk Franklin, *First Love*, which says, "He is able to heal if you listen. Come back to your first love." This is a great song. Kirk shares that if you have made mistakes in your life, you can always come back home and God will heal all your wounds, remove all of your suffering. All you have to do is listen to the Lord and follow the road home.

The aforementioned birthrights are just a few of the promises, blessings, and gifts the Lord has in store for you.

The Father promises you life to the full (John 10:10); a long life (1 Kings 3:14); deliverance from all your troubles (Ps. 34:19); all your needs will be met (Phil. 4:19); and a prize for staying faithful until the end (1 Cor. 9:24, Phil. 3:14).

God has promised you many more gifts and blessings than I could ever hope to write about. However, read the Scriptures carefully because each promise is delivered upon the steadfastness of your faith, the depth of your love for him, and your endurance throughout your spiritual journey.

Deepen Your Personal Convictions

Read: 1 Peter 1:3-7; Ephesians 1:18-19; Colossians 1:9-14; Colossians 3:23-24

1. What is a birthright?

2. How does God's inheritance apply to you?

3. What is the best way to use your spiritual inheritance?

4. Pray daily to embrace your birthright and believe in its power in your life.

CHAPTER 5
The Designer's Plan

I know what I'm doing. I have it planned out–plans to take care of you, not abandon you, plans to give you the future you hope for. When you call on me, when you come and pray to me, I'll listen. When you come looking for me, you'll find me. Yes, when you get serious about finding me and want it more than anything else, I'll make sure you won't be disappointed. GOD'S Decree.

(Jer. 29:11-14, THE MESSAGE)

Jeremiah 29:11-14 has inspired me for more than twelve years. I get goose bumps knowing the Lord thinks about me and that since the beginning of time he has had specific plans just for me. This promise is for every woman created by God.

Even before you were born, the Father had specific and detailed plans for you; like an expecting mother who dreams of what she will do with her daughter, where she will take her child, what her child will become, and how much she already loves her daughter. However, God doesn't simply dream, he already *knows* what the earthly mother dreams of for her child. His *visions* created you, and if you allow it, his *visions* and *precepts* will guide you to heaven and eternity.

Ask yourself, why would God create *his masterpiece* only to leave it to fend for itself without any protection, nourishment, or purpose? He wouldn't! God has provided for you in ways you don't even realize. The Lord is diligent in making sure you have everything you need to survive and so many of the things you want.

The key to God's plan is trusting in it. As a sinner you are fearful, skeptical, independent, prideful, and rebellious. As a human you think, "How can I trust a plan I have not designed myself? How do I trust a plan where many of the details are a mystery?" Sister, all I can say is this…with deep and continual prayer.

Standing by faith is difficult in times of uncertainty, hardship, and loss. Yet God calls you to rely upon him and his plan. In Jeremiah 29:13 (NIV), after God tells you he has a plan for you, he then says that you *will* find him when you seek him with *all* of your heart. So if you are confused by God's plan or don't trust it, the question I have for you is…"Are you wholeheartedly seeking the Lord?"

When you seek the Lord with no resistance in your heart, his plan becomes clearer. The details unfold as you mature in your Christian journey, yet there will always be an air of mystery as in any good story that unfolds before the reader's eyes.

You will only be able to understand the Lord's plans when you are seeking him with everything you have, your entire heart, mind, body, and soul; anything less causes confusion, doubt, disappointment, mistrust, impatience, anxiety, hopelessness, loneliness, rebellion, and ultimately sin.

When I have wholeheartedly sought after the Lord, and put aside all doubt, I have *never* been disappointed. He is faithful, and surely the Creator of the Universe can do anything my simple mind requests.

So you ask, "What is God's plan for me?" God's plan includes:

- Developing a strong faith that God exists and he earnestly works for the good of those who love him (Rom. 8:28).
- Pursuing a deep and meaningful personal relationship with the Lord.
- Asking the Lord to forgive the sins you have already committed against him and to forgive the sins you commit daily.
- Forgiving those who have sinned against you.
- Loving the people in your life, including strangers and enemies.
- Avoiding the sinful schemes of this world.
- Sacrificing yourself so God can be glorified.
- Diligently working through conflicts with a humble and loving heart.
- Remaining hopeful that the Father will get you through even the darkest of times.
- Sharing his Word with others.

I wish I could give you details that are more specific to you. I cannot. I do know God wants you to be with him, living an abundant life as you fulfill his mission. I can share with you four certainties from Jeremiah:

1. God has a plan specifically for you.
2. When you pray to him, he will listen.
3. You will find him when you seek him with all of your heart.
4. You will not be disappointed when you put your full trust in him.

There is a myth in the pseudo-Christian and non-Christian world that following God's plan means you have to give up every personal dream you've ever had. That is false! God didn't make you creative and ambitious so you could stuff those traits and bury them inside of your heart. It is true that as you align yourself with God your priorities change. Your first priority will be to please God. If you give up a dream it is because it no longer fits with your godly priorities and desires.

The Father is asking you to honor him with your life while you pursue your dreams and goals. God is asking you to change your sinful nature and embrace his characteristics that he gave you. He is *not* asking you to give up the spirit of who you are. I have found that it is easier to achieve my goals with God at my side. I am able to embrace the best parts of me and live a life that is fulfilling and allows me to help others. So stop believing you have to change everything about yourself to the point of not recognizing who you are.

Sometimes, it is challenging to follow God's plan. Yet I am certain his plan will fill you up to overflowing, as you embrace his love and goodwill. The Lord knows the desires of your heart and wants you to be happy. If you do things *his* way, you will be blessed eternally.

When I am confused about how to please God, I stop for a moment, pray, and ask myself what would God want me to do? How can I honor God in this situation? You can please the Lord and still achieve what is important to you like taking care of your family, finishing school, making new friends, dating, getting married, asking your boss for a raise, or starting a business. The Bible says that if you delight yourself in the Lord he will give you the desires of your heart (Ps. 37:4), and if you ask for things in his name, you shall receive them (John 16:24), as long as you do not doubt your faith and the power and grace of God (Matt. 21:21-22).

I am certain God's principles are right and that they work, yet it takes great focus to follow them. As for you, Sister, the best thing you can do when you doubt God's infinite wisdom and plan, or you want to rely on yourself, is to pray for trust in the Lord and follow him. Call a spiritual friend who will hold you accountable to God's principles, and then pray again.

I challenge you to think through an area of your life where you find yourself doubting the Lord and make a decision to follow God's principle on the issue. If you are uncertain about what God says about your situation, pray for clarity and call your spiritual friend to examine the Scriptures together. Buy a Bible concordance and study out what God says. The Bible is useful for *every* area of your life (2 Tim. 3:16). When you seek God wholeheartedly, you *will* find the answer.

James 1:6-8 says we must believe and not doubt, for those who doubt are like waves tossed back and forth by the wind, double-minded and uncertain. Surely frustration and anxiety haunt the woman who doubts the power of

God. And although doubt may happen at some time in your life, *you cannot stay* in that state of confusion.

The designer's plan for you is timeless. His plan involves love and forgiveness. He will bless your faith and grant you salvation. Your sacrifice and self-discipline will be rewarded as you pursue endeavors that honor the Lord and advance his kingdom. The Father wants you to think of him first in everything you do and look for ways to please him with your life. And as you seek after God your heart will be filled with hope, peace, and joy. Place your trust in the Lord and watch his miracles unfold in your life and in the lives of the people you touch.

Deepen Your Personal Convictions

Read: Luke 19:1-10; Acts 17:24-27

1. What does Luke 19 say about why Jesus came to the Earth?

2. What does Acts 17 say about your life?

3. Why are you seeking the Lord?

4. How are you seeking the Lord with *all* of your heart?

5. Pray daily for God's plan for your life to be clear to you and for his will to be done in your life.

CHAPTER 6

Spiritual Royalty

But you are a chosen people, a royal priesthood, a holy nation, a people belonging to God, that you may declare the praises of him who called you out of darkness into his wonderful light.

(1 Pet. 2:9)

The time has come for me to dispel any wrong thinking about what a *Divine Princess* is.

In the world we view a princess as wealthy, beautiful, thin, famous, and flawless. She is waited on hand-and-foot, living in a lavish palace surrounded by the finest things. She is a socialite: totally feminine, having exquisite taste, graceful movements, proper speech, and impeccable manners. She wears expensive, designer clothes and is adorned with precious jewels. She received her education from the most prestigious institutions. She has everything! She's Royal Barbie.

We believe worldly royals have it all. Their lives overflow with glamour, fun, excitement, and mystery. They never grow tired or old, and their lives are a utopia of ease. This is a distorted view of worldly royalty and does not even come close to depicting spiritual royalty. So let me set the record straight about the life of a *fearfully and wonderfully made woman* of God.

Every woman on the planet is destined to become a *Divine Princess* simply because she has been created by God for his purpose. However, the fulfillment of your *divine* destiny depends upon the choices you make in your life. A woman who has chosen to follow the Lord is a *Divine Princess*. Her inheritance has been secured by the blood of Jesus and cannot be questioned. So your birthright, as a daughter to The King, is freely yours to behold. *How* you are living your life determines if you understand, believe in, and embrace your *divinity*. Ephesians 4:1-3 urges you to "live a life worthy of the calling you have received" and "make every effort" to be united to the Spirit of Christ. Are you living a life worthy of The King? Are you making ***every effort*** to be united to Christ, your Lord? That is your destiny!

A woman who has embraced her *divinity* is living a life that is "holy and pleasing to God" as her "spiritual act of worship" to the Lord. She no longer follows the patterns of this world, but has transformed her mind and heart to align with God (Rom. 12:1-2).

A *divine* life is not comprised of the things you may envision when you think of worldly royalty. A woman pursuing a *divine* life has heavenly aspirations and considers first the principles of God, then with humility and gratitude receives the blessings *divine* living produces.

A woman who has embraced her *divinity*:

- does not strive for perfection, but instead strives to be like Jesus.
- might be a loving wife and mother, or have no living biological family to lavish her love upon, yet she turns to God for unconditional love and in return shares that love with others.
- may have numerous friends or just one best friend, yet she strives to be a great friend: loving, honest, spiritual, supportive, and fun.
- might be famous and recognizable by many or she might be invisible to some, yet she believes her Father in heaven always sees her and values how she feels.
- knows she is beautiful whether she has creamy white skin or skin the richest shade of brown. She does not compare herself to others because she remembers she is a unique masterpiece and no others compare to her in the eyes of the Lord.
- strives to maintain or enhance her outer appearance, yet she knows her inner beauty is most important to the Lord.

- always identifies with the family of God, even though she may be Irish, Jamaican, Greek, Chinese, Peruvian, German, Vietnamese, African, Canadian, Mexican, English, Australian, East Indian, Hawaiian, or from the Southern United States.
- is proud of her biological culture and heritage, yet holds her head high as spiritual royalty…as a daughter of The King.
- humbly asserts herself as the *divine* daughter of God, setting healthy boundaries in relationships while serving others as Jesus would.
- may live in a spacious mansion or a simple apartment, yet her heart always resides with her Father.
- may own an expensive SUV and shop on Rodeo Drive in Beverly Hills, or she may ride public transportation and frequent her neighborhood Goodwill store. Yet, she knows the value of her clothes, home, and car do not determine her value as a woman created by the most innovative and talented designer of all.
- realizes no level of education—formal or informal—will get her to heaven, yet she values education in all forms and believes being a great student of the Lord produces timeless wisdom and heavenly fruit.

The past of a Divine Princess may:

- include growing up in the church, or she may have never even cracked open a Bible as a child or young adult.

- be like pure snow or colored with a myriad of impure and immoral escapades.
- be brimming over with lies, drunkenness, cursing, theft, drugs, violence, or even jail time.
- shine with self-confidence and demonstrations of her unique abilities, or she may have spent her teen years following the crowd and putting herself down at every opportunity.
- be darkened by desperate flirting and sexual promiscuity, or she may have been the victim of rape or incest.
- include ideal emotional, physical, and mental health, or she may have suffered from postpartum depression or cancer, or lack the full use of her arms.

A woman who has embraced her *divinity* does not let her past transgressions or current situation hold her back from living a life that pleases the Lord.

A Divine Princess chooses to:

- imitate the character of Jesus.
- speak the truth with love, minding her tongue, so she encourages rather than destroys the people around her.
- turn to God to rid her spirit of bitterness, anger, impatience, fear, greed, jealousy, hatred, anxiety, and impurity.
- align her values with those of the Lord to develop her character to become more like Jesus.
- utilize the values of God as her personal measuring stick and not the misguided beliefs of society and other people.

- acknowledge her sins and work diligently to be consumed with the things of the Lord and not the things of Satan and this world.
- apologize quickly for her sinful nature rather than blame others for her failures.
- avoid situations where old temptations lie waiting to destroy her.
- see herself through the eyes of God and not dwell on her previous distorted image of herself, nor the latest fashion magazines and the disturbing views of bewildered youth.
- rely on God to fill her with strength, courage, and a will to live abundantly.
- value her body and mind as a temple of the Lord.
- believe in the sanctity of marriage as God instituted and obey the principles of the Lord for pure dating and godly relationships.
- follow the Bible as her standard for living and pursue a life that is worthy of the calling she has received from the Lord.

Having said all that, a *Divine Princess* is *divine* because she beholds God's character in her heart and has *chosen* to make Jesus the Lord of her life (Rom. 10:9-13). Yet she is not perfect or sin free. She *will* sin. In fact, at this very moment a *Divine Princess* is doing something sinful, like arguing with her husband, or having an attitude towards her boss, or being impatient with her children. Yet, when she realizes her sin she turns to her relationship with the Lord to strengthen her and create in her godly repentance (2 Cor. 7:9b-11).

Ultimately, a *Divine Princess* who has embraced her *divinity* consistently strives to obey God's commands.

Through her dedication to the Lord, she continues to grow spiritually and turns her failures into successes and learning opportunities. She uses the Bible and her experiences to help others grow closer to Christ.

So if are you tired of pursuing the unfulfilling passions of this world and tired of relying on men and others who continually hurt and disappoint you, devote yourself to Jesus. Know that no matter where you find yourself today, Jesus loves you, and can heal every wound and scar you have. Keep reading as I share my story with you and the stories of two *Divine Sisters*. Each story will give you perspective and help you understand how you can turn from sin and live a life holy and pleasing to God as his *Divine Princess*.

Deepen Your Personal Convictions

Read: Philippians 1:27-28; 1 Timothy 4:16; Ephesians 4:28-5:7

1. Do you believe you are a daughter to The King? Why or why not?

2. Do you believe you are a *Divine Princess*? Why or why not?

3. Are you embracing your *divinity* on a daily basis? Why or why not?

4. How can embracing your *divinity* daily change your life?

5. Pray daily for God to be your personal measuring stick. Pray to humbly recognize where you need to make changes in your life to embrace God more deeply.

CHAPTER 7
The Struggle Within

So I find this law at work: When I want to do good, evil is right there with me. For in my inner being I delight in God's law; but I see another law at work in the members of my body, waging war against the law of my mind and making me a prisoner of the law of sin at work within my members. What a wretched [wo]man I am. Who will rescue me from this body of death?
(Rom. 7:21-24)

If you are anything like me your past and possibly your present are littered with too many sins to count or recall.

I grew up in a two bedroom, one bath home in San Francisco, California. We had six people living in my house: my dad, whom I could go three to four days without even seeing; my mom, who is loving and supportive, yet very short on discipline; my two sisters, who are very different for legitimate reasons; my great-grandmother, who helped raise me until she died when I was seventeen; and me, the middle child with ambition, independence, and an obvious dislike for the word "No!"

When I was a little girl, like many girls, I dreamt about being a princess, marrying a prince, and living happily ever after. I remember pretending to be a princess. I watched every fairytale and dreamt I was the maiden in distress who was rescued by the handsome and very rich prince living in a kingdom he would one day inherit. We would have children who would be beautiful, smart, perfect, and somehow contribute to world peace. Then I grew up without God, started to date, and my dream of being a princess quickly faded. I sacrificed my dream, convictions, body, and soul for false security and temporary love in ways I am ashamed of and have been hesitant to talk or write about.

I remember feeling disappointed, sad, and at times lonely as my dream of royalty, marrying a prince, perfect children, and world peace slipped away.

I cringe when I think about the ugly things I have done over the years. Desperate flirting, promiscuity, abortions, and even adultery (as the "other woman") darken my past. I started going to clubs at age fourteen and drinking and smoking in middle school. By the time I got to college I had been around the block a *few* times.

In terms of sex outside of marriage, I would tell my friends, "You have to try the shoe on first to see if it fits before you buy it." In high school, I even encouraged some of my fourteen and fifteen year old girlfriends to have sex with their boyfriends. (Aaahhhh!) As a parent of a fifteen-year-old-daughter, I beg God daily she does not fall into the same sins I fell into as a young girl (and that she does not have friends like the old me).

My past is not perfect and full of light as I wish it were. In fact, there are more instances than I care to recall that are nowhere near *divine*.

By the grace of God, my life changed! I came to truly love Jesus and his Kingdom in 1996, yet I still did not completely understand my value to God, my spiritual inheritance, or my role as a daughter of The King.

Understanding your value to God as a woman is crucial for embracing your *divinity*. The great thing is there is always hope and God never gives up on you. Every day you wake up you have another opportunity to choose God. Any moment you are faced with a decision, you can choose God.

When I became a true Christian there were many things I just stopped doing, like cursing, getting drunk, flirting with men, lying, and stealing to name a few. However, it took me several years to understand the depth of being a daughter of Christ.

Today, I am still amazed by his power. Understanding my self-worth according to God, and not the world, fills me with love, joy, peace, hope, and power.

So many days I feel indestructible, like the world is my oyster, and every opportunity is within my reach. I want you to feel the same way. More importantly God wants you to feel his love, hope, and power knowing that with him all things are possible (Mark 10:27).

I wrote Chapters 6, 7, and 8 so you would have a clearer understanding not just of what a *Divine Princess* is, but also *how* a *Divine Princess* should live her life. It is also important that you know that your past sins do not have to stop you from living as a *Divine Princess* today and from this day forward.

Everyone sins (Rom. 3:23). Everyday there is a battle going on inside of me to do evil or to do good. Fortunately, I have Jesus and the Holy Spirit to help me make godly choices. I blow it often (just ask my husband and children). I'm not striving to be perfect; I'm striving to be like Jesus. When "I fix my eyes on Jesus, the author and perfecter of my faith" (Heb. 12:2), I please God. God doesn't expect perfection from me or from you. He expects your love, repentance, and obedience. He expects you to strive to be like Jesus—pure and holy. He knows you will sin and make mistakes. Yet your humility, gratefulness, and love for him will cause you to repent, turn away from sin, and follow him with a willing heart.

I know Christianity can be hard. I know it can seem overwhelming at times. But that is what Satan wants you to believe—that you can't do it. But you can. Satan is wrong. God is right! Even if you are surrounded by people who are involved in sinful pursuits, making it that much harder for you to follow Christ, you can do it. I know watching them makes it easier for you to justify or dismiss your sin saying, "Well, everyone else is doing it." But just because your friend jumps off a bridge are you gonna do it too? (Do I sound like your mama? 'Cause I know I sound like mine.)

Jesus understands the world is full of temptations and yet he knows you can avoid them. He believes you can train yourself (like an athlete or student) to turn away from sin and be godly. Jesus is your protector. When you are weak and admit you need Christ that is when you become strong. In those moments you are empowered to overcome any struggle and sin in your life.

So if you are currently steeped in sin, repent, turn to him, and obey his commands. You are not alone in the struggle, nor in the joy of following God. In the seventh chapter of Romans, Paul goes into detail about how the sin he wishes not to do, he keeps on doing, and struggles to do the good he wants to do. He asks who can rescue him from the bondage of sin. The answer is Jesus. Jesus rescued Paul, he rescued me, and he can rescue you from the bondage of sin.

> Even to your old age and gray hairs I am he, I am he who will sustain you. I have made you and I will carry you; I will sustain you and I will rescue you.
>
> (Isa. 46:4)

Jesus will never give up on you. And with him the world is your oyster, so keep reading to find your way home…to the Father's palace.

Deepen Your Personal Convictions

Read: Galatians 5:19-21; Romans 7:14-25

1. What sins are you struggling with at this point in your life?

2. Can you relate to how Paul was feeling? How? Be specific?

3. Are you looking for someone to rescue you from your sinful ways?

4. Pray daily for Jesus Christ to rescue you from the sin surrounding you.

CHAPTER 8

Lessons from a Divine Sister

Blessed is she who has believed that what the Lord has said to her will be accomplished!

(Luke 1:45)

You have many sisters who have come before you that have embraced their *divinity*; sisters whose lives started out less than *divine*. From their examples you can learn many, many valuable lessons. Although there are several sisters in Scripture I could have highlighted, I chose two sisters from the New Testament whose brief stories in the Bible are packed with compelling examples of hope, courage, faith, trust, and action.

Before you read any further in this book, grab your Bible and read the account of The Woman Who Lived a Sinful Life in Luke 7:36-50. She is a *Divine Princess*.

Read Her Story

When I read about The Woman Who Lived a Sinful Life I am encouraged by her humility, faith, and actions. I feel humbled to have something in common with her. I have lived a sinful life. Many things I did in my past were ugly. I prostituted my body. Maybe not in the traditional way of selling sex for money, but I have given myself away to more boys and men than I can remember. It hurts to share that.

I want you to notice several things about her story. Notice the Bible never mentions her name. It never says what sins she has actually committed, yet because of the time period in which she lived, her sins probably included prostitution, adultery, or some form of sexual immorality. The Woman never speaks, never opens her mouth. Everything she expresses to Jesus she communicates through her actions. Throughout the entire passage she remains in a position of humility and service (most likely on her knees, briefly, if ever, looking into Jesus' eyes or into the eyes of the other men staring at her).

I am humbled just writing about her. Take a moment to ponder this sinful woman's situation and actions. What was going through her mind? Was she scared? Did she feel the eyes of those around her penetrating her skin, seeing only the sin she was in and not the depth of her soul? Could she hear the men talking about her? Did she feel judged or loved by Jesus?

Now, please read about the Woman Who Bled for Twelve Years in Mark 5:24-34. She is a *Divine Princess*.

Read Her Story

Notice again, the Bible never mentions her name. Her actions lead to her blessing. She also portrays humility by not seeking the direct attention of Jesus; she *just* wants to touch his cloak. She has committed no sin that places her in this painful, humiliating, and lonely situation. Her faith amazes me! Her desperation scares me and causes me sadness. Have you ever been desperate? I mean *really* desperate? I have.

I am afraid to share my story with you. Yet, I do so in an effort to connect with you and let you know you are not alone in the fight against Satan.

When I was sixteen I had an abortion. I had been having sex without protection for over a year and eventually luck was no longer on my side. Fear seized every inch of my being when I realized I was pregnant. I knew my father would kill me!

At the time I told only three people—my best friend, my older sister, and one of the two boys I was dating. (I am getting lightheaded just sharing about my past.)

I decided to have an abortion because I could never have told my parents I was pregnant. In addition, my selfishness kicked in and I could only envision the beating I would receive at home, my future which I considered bright, and how I had no means of caring responsibly for a child. I remember *begging* God to help me. Now I wasn't a Christian, nor was I behaving *divinely*. Yet I begged for God to help me. I didn't ask, I begged. I wept for hours. I cried out desperately to the Lord. I made a deal with God that if he rescued me I would never do this (have another abortion) again. I feared what God's answer to my prayer would be. I feared his reprisal for my sin. I hated myself for what I was doing to my body and to my baby.

Unfortunately, my story gets worse before it gets better. In my ignorance, selfishness, and downright rebellion, I continued to sleep around and four years later I found myself pregnant again. This time I remembered my promise to God and decided to keep this baby, even though I was unmarried and uncertain of how to care for a child. I refused to have an abortion. So many times I have wished I had made that same strong stand against having sex outside of marriage.

Since I was willing to be impure, but not a murderer (again), I continued having sex. Of course, eight months after my daughter was born, I discovered I was pregnant for a third time.

I remember it clearly, it was August 1993, I was twenty-two years old, unmarried, not a Christian, in college full-time, working part-time, and I felt my plate was full. I could not picture myself as the mother of two small children; patience was not my strong suit. Parenting was hard...especially as an unwed mother. My daughter's father, who is now my husband, was actively involved in our life, and I *was* enjoying my new baby. She was beautiful, and God gave her a temperament I could handle. Yet, I knew I did not want another child. So, even after I had promised God I would never have another abortion…I did.

I walked into the doctor's office for that second abortion feeling grieved to my very soul. I could hardly speak. I cried quietly as the procedure was done and I felt numb all over my body. Afterwards, I fled the city, hoping that running away would make the guilt and pain disappear. It didn't. I cried out to God to forgive me. I desperately wanted him to forgive me, but I thought he never would. How could he after what I'd done. I had chosen not to keep the promise I had made to him six years earlier. In addition, I had committed again what I believe in God's eyes is murder.

Guilt…shame…and loneliness overwhelmed me.

My nature is to shake off negative feelings—to bypass my sin quickly and act like it hasn't happened. So after three days in hiding, I returned to my life and pretended like nothing had happened. I was afraid of God. I feared I would slip into an eternal depression if I thought too much about how deeply I had hurt myself, my babies, and the Lord. So I chose to ignore my sin. I buried the thoughts of my babies, the abortions, and my shame deep within my mind. I refused to talk about it.

Sad thing is...some things completely tragic, like abortion and murder, haunt you. They torment your soul. The shame and guilt didn't disappear just because I wanted to bury my head in the sand. Satan still fills me with guilt, shame, and self-hatred, when I think about it all these years later. I did not do what I knew was right. I know Jesus has forgiven me. Yet, the "what ifs" haunt me on days I dwell on what I did.

In a different way I was in pain like the Woman Who Bled. Her story is impacting for many of the same reasons as the Sinful Woman. In reading about these two women

I hope you are inspired more than anything else, knowing Jesus provided them with peace, love, forgiveness and salvation. You can glean many lessons from their situations.

The Sinful Woman experienced desperation, as well. She felt desperate for real love. She felt desperate for forgiveness. She was worn out and discouraged by the life she had been living. She needed to be healed. She needed to be accepted and considered as a person, valuable... with feelings, thoughts, and talents. *You know,* she had to be scared to enter Simon's home. He despised everything about her. In her humility she was greeted by ridicule and criticism. The searing eyes of the men present stung with each step she took. She felt their hatred for her and her lifestyle. She sought one man, Jesus, to show her compassion and grant her forgiveness of her many sins. This Sinful Woman risked being beaten and imprisoned to behold Jesus—the one who could rescue her. At all costs, she committed herself to being near the Lord, the one she had only heard about...the Savior!

The Woman Who Bled was bold and courageous, yet frightened and willing to risk someone noticing her illness. During biblical times, bleeding was considered an unclean act. So everything she touched was considered unclean. People looked down on her and she was ostracized by them because of her illness.

Unfortunately, the Woman Who Bled had no control over her situation. Nothing she had done had caused her illness. The Bible does not mention any sin that she had committed. Yet she suffered everyday with pain, loneliness, and rejection. Doctors took all her money and subjected her to treatments that caused her more pain than relief. Nowhere else to turn, she sought the Lord.

She heard about Jesus and knew she had to find him. She wholeheartedly believed in his power. She had to. She had tried everything else. So she exposed herself to public humiliation to finally be healed.

These women displayed many characteristics of a *Divine Princess* and God allowed their stories to be in the Bible to encourage and inspire women everywhere—women like you and me, in any situation.

Each Woman Had Immeasurable Hope

Hope! God also placed in you immeasurable hope. Each page you read of this book says you have hope. Each action you take says you have hope. Each tear you shed says, "Lord, please give me hope." Each time you yell says, "I don't want to lose hope!" Each time you keep silent when you really want to speak says, "Please, hope, don't leave me." The Sinful Woman had hope. She believed the Lord would love her, even though she was a sinner. The Woman Who Bled had hope. She believed the Lord would heal her and make her suffering stop. Hope is kept alive in your heart by that deep-seated (sometimes unconscious) desire to be with Jesus.

Aaaah, hope! That whisper that repeats again and again, "There's got to be something more." Just wait, it's coming. Close your eyes. Quiet your mind. Tune out your surroundings and listen for the whispering. It's there. It's always there. Hope. Do you hear it prodding you to never give up? The voice of hope is Jesus calling you to come and place your burdens with him.

Each Woman Displayed Great Courage

The Sinful Woman risked her life going into Simon's home where she was not welcome. The Woman Who Bled risked public humiliation. They refused to allow fear to stop them from pursuing the Lord.

> Courage is not the absence of fear, but rather the judgment that something else is more important than fear.
>
> (Ambrose Redmoon)

Each knew her healing was far more important than her fear. Their courage is impressive and another powerful example of the strength of woman.

Summon your courage to help you persevere in times of struggle. Summon your courage to go against the grain; to rise above the crowd; to step out of your comfort zone and let your light shine.

Each Woman Had Great Faith

Each of these women believed the Lord was her salvation. Jesus…there to save her, forgive her, love her, protect her, cherish her, and renew her spirit. Jesus, the Lord, told each woman go in peace, your faith has saved you…healed you (Luke 7:50; Mark 5:34). They are forever remembered in the Bible because of their astounding faith.

> Without faith it is impossible to please God, because anyone who comes to him must believe he exists and that he rewards those who earnestly seek him.
>
> (Heb. 11:6)

Both of these *Divine Princesses* risked their lives to be healed. Jesus was moved by their faith and blessed each woman with the cure for her pain. Each embraced her *divinity*, and in doing so each woman pleased God and was rewarded for her faith.

What is the condition of your faith today? God says with only a mustard seed of faith nothing will be impossible for you (Matt. 17:20-21). A mustard seed is as small as one letter on this page. All you need is a mustard seed size amount of faith to conquer your sin and fear, and to live with the Father. Surely, God Almighty, the Creator of the Universe, who would never leave you defenseless, has bestowed upon you enough strength to produce faith the size of a mustard seed.

Each Woman Trusted in the Lord's Power

I'll admit each woman had the advantage of living when Jesus lived. She had heard of his miracles, maybe even seen one first hand or seen the product of his work in her neighbor who had been healed. So in some sense it may make trusting in Jesus' power easier. Make no mistake though, Jesus is powerful even if you ignore the miracles being performed today.

As I was writing this book, I was told the story of a young girl, who fell several stories from her apartment window.

> Angel (names have been changed to protect identity) was looking at a dog below when the screen gave way and she fell…nine stories to the ground. Her mother, Margo, happened to be outside the building saying goodbye to some friends who had visited them. As Margo watched the friends walk away she heard a loud thud behind her in the grass. When Margo turned she heard her older daughter, Bethany, scream Angel's name from the ninth floor. Fear swept over Margo as she turned and ran toward the sound of the thud.
>
> As Margo approached the building she saw Angel's limp, lifeless body lying there on her face. She scooped Angel up into her arms and began screaming out

to God, "Lord, have mercy! Lord, have mercy!" As Margo was repeating her plea to God, Angel's eyes popped open, yet she was very still. The neighbors heard Margo's screams and called an ambulance. A few minutes later Bethany appeared outside. She was out of breath because she had run down the stairs from the ninth floor. Bethany began to pray, as well.

Angel was taken to the hospital. There Margo sent out calls and pleas to everyone she knew asking for prayers of a miracle. The friends and family members who received the calls were stunned. They prayed, but with very little optimism as they saw no way a child could survive a fall from that height. After a full examination, CAT Scan, MRI, and numerous other tests from a team of doctors, Angel was found to have no broken bones, no concussion, no internal bleeding, and although she fell on her face, she only had one tiny cut on her chin. She had landed on the only patch of grass near the building. A miracle had occurred. Angel had survived with no brain damage and no permanent injury. She amazed doctors. She amazed her family and friends.

Angel's story inspires my faith. She is a miracle of Jesus. Despite the lack of faith found in the prayers that went out to Jesus, he still saw fit to protect/heal this child. The one thing that really struck me about this family was their devotion to Jesus. Only Margo was a Christian before the accident. She faithfully followed the Lord's principles. Margo and her two daughters prayed at every opportunity, even meal times, for her husband, Bob, to become a Christian, too. It took a true miracle, this miracle, for Bob to study the Bible, trust in God's power, repent of his sins, get baptized, and commit his life to Christ. Be sure Angel and Bethany will both become Christians one day, because of Margo's trust in the power of the Lord. This mother, this woman, your *Divine Sister,* put her trust in the Lord and he performed not one, but two great miracles in her life: her daughter's protection from a deadly fall, and her husband's rebirth as a Christian.

What can you learn from Margo, whose daughter should have been killed by that fall from the ninth story? How did she show trust? She prayed. Her simple prayer showed faith and trust in the Lord that he would listen and answer. She believed that "the prayer of a righteous [wo]man is powerful and effective" (James 5:16). She sought the prayers of her family and friends, hoping to move God's heart to save her child. I believed it worked. God performed a miracle because his daughter called out to him in desperation when she needed him most. God felt her pain.

When my oldest daughter was three years old she choked on a large piece of hard candy. It was Valentine's Day 1996. I would get baptized four days later. I am reminded of this event, because I felt my daughter's life was in jeopardy and I cried out to God. I was in my bedroom getting ready for work when I heard Ajya choking from another room. I stopped what I was doing and listened. She was making a horrible gurgling sound. I ran to her as she was running to me. She pointed to her throat. I scooped her up just like Margo with her small child. I flipped her upside down and ran to the kitchen to get the phone. I had taken infant CPR and even though Ajya was probably too old for that, it was all I could remember at that moment.

As I was dialing 9-1-1, I began calling out to the Lord, "Not to today, Lord! Not today, Lord! Not today!" Ajya was still choking when the 9-1-1 operator answered the phone. I clumsily told her what was happening and tried to focus on her questions about my address and if Ajya could breathe or talk. I remember the anxiety I felt as I considered life without my baby. Again, I implored God to spare her life and show us mercy.

When I realized what the 9-1-1 operator was asking me, I turned Ajya over and asked her a question. She responded. "Hallelujah!" went through my mind. She seemed to be able to breathe even though this huge piece of candy was lodged in her tiny throat. By the time the Paramedics arrived, Ajya had swallowed the candy. God had performed a miracle. I had trusted in God, even though I wasn't a Christian yet I was seeking the Lord with all of my heart. I had called on God and he answered my cry for help…again.

The Woman Who Bled and the Sinful Woman each put her trust in Jesus' power to heal her. Each woman trusted that the stories about Jesus were true—he was the Messiah, the Savior, come to provide healing and bring the message of God.

Trust is the foundation of every great relationship. Even though Jesus isn't standing in front of you today, you can be like these women. Notice the everyday miracles around you: a woman is healed from breast cancer; a child escapes a predator; a person survives a car accident; and a woman turns her life over to Jesus.

Ponder the mysteries of the Earth. How does the sun rise and set each day? How does your brain function, and know to pump blood through every part of your body? How come the trees provide you with the oxygen you need and you can turn oxygen into carbon dioxide, which is what the trees need? Who set that up? Better yet, who keeps it going?

God performs all theses miracles and many more everyday. Let's not take them for granted.

Each Woman Took Simple Action

Faith without action is dead (James 2:26). If either the Sinful Woman or the Woman Who Bled had decided to stay at home sulking, telling herself she was unworthy, or making busy with housework, or worrying about something that hadn't even happened, she would have missed her opportunity to be saved and healed from her emotional and physical suffering. Each took her desire for love, forgiveness, and salvation out of her home and on to the scary, often unwelcoming, and lonely road to find Jesus.

Each put her faith into practice, one with tears and a jar of perfume; the other with a single brush of her hand—simple actions that resulted in great blessings.

What simple action are you willing to take to be healed? Although Scripture says you cannot work your way into heaven, God does expect you to take action. You cannot sit passively by and allow salvation to escape you. You must take action. Do it today!

Each Woman is You and Someone You Know and Love

I believe each woman is never named because it allows you to see yourself more clearly in her story. If it were Deborah, or Esther, or Mary, you might say, I could never be like that, or that's *her* story, mine is different. Yet as the stories are now, when you peer deep into this woman's soul, you see your image and realize that she is you. She is someone you know. It is your mother, sister, daughter, best friend, or neighbor. It is your coworker, the wife of your child's soccer coach, or the clerk at your grocery store. These stories are relatable to you and many women you know and love.

Each Woman was Changed Forever

One simple action led to a miracle for each woman. No story is more powerful than a woman who has been steeped in sin, pain, and bitterness; who has struggled to survive, and then miraculously she is saved from darkness and her suffering.

Maybe you don't feel as desperate as one of these women, or maybe you do. Either way, do not minimize or discount your suffering, which reminds you of your need for Jesus.

As a *Divine Princess* the Lord will give you his spirit, his power to carry Immeasurable Hope in your heart, display Great Courage, Trust in his Power, have Great Faith, and take Simple Action. You know this woman because she is you. You want change in some area of your life and with Jesus you can have lasting and magnificent change in *every* area of your life. It just takes Hope, Courage, Faith, Trust, and Action; everything God has already given to you. Each of these rests within your heart waiting to be released by your deliberate reliance on God's power and not on your own.

Deepen Your Personal Convictions

Read: Luke 7:36-50; Mark 5:24-34

1. Which *Divine Sister* had the most impact on your heart? Why?

2. What two things did you learn from the stories of your *Divine Sisters*?

3. What simple actions will you take to seek the Lord?

4. Pray daily to follow through with simple actions that lead you closer to Jesus.

CHAPTER 9

Glorious Inner Strength

I ask him to strengthen you by his Spirit—not a brute strength but a glorious inner strength—that Christ will live in you as you open the door and invite him in. And I ask him that with both feet planted firmly on love, you'll be able to take in with all Christians the extravagant dimensions of Christ's love.

(Eph. 3:16-18, THE MESSAGE)

When I think about women today I have mixed feelings. I feel like now more than ever we need Jesus. So many women are troubled, frustrated, lonely, desperate, and abused emotionally, verbally, and physically. Yet, I also feel like we have come a long way. We just had one of the most successful runs for the presidency of the United States by a woman. She ran a good campaign and many thought she would be the next president of the United States. And even though something so incredible can happen for a woman in the U.S., our world is still plagued by sexism, sexual harassment, discrimination, and misogynistic attitudes and behaviors toward women. Magazines, television, radio, music, and books still display women as objects—toys to be played with and discarded when one no longer has a use for them.

How sad God must be every time he looks upon the earth and sees how women are treated and portrayed. We are his brilliant, bold, and beautiful masterpiece and yet too often treated like objects with no thoughts, feelings, or talents outside the bedroom. It's even more painful because women allow themselves to be disrespected and treated like mindless sex toys. It is time we stood up and took our rightful place in this world—the one God created for us. It's time we love and respect ourselves the way God loves us. I'm not necessarily talking about an uprising of women, but surely taking a personal and collective stand against being treated like trash, being taken advantage of, and being abused.

I don't mean to imply nothing is being done to right the wrongs against women. Yet, if we truly loved ourselves and saw ourselves as God's masterpiece, we would think differently, behave differently, and expect different things for our lives. We would pursue godly endeavors. We wouldn't allow ourselves to be portrayed as sluts and dim wits and then paraded around as objects with no thoughts, feelings, or talents. If we really believed in our *divinity* we would not tolerate misogynistic attitudes and behaviors toward women. We would expect better from ourselves, our husbands, families, children, friends, employers, teachers, and role models, and even strangers.

However, there are still far too many women who passively allow society and those around them to dictate who they are. Society would have you believe you are only valuable and pretty if you are blonde, blue-eyed, Caucasian, 5'9", 115 lbs, with a C-cup, perfect bone structure, full lips and cheeks, and no wrinkles or cellulite.

Let me ask you a question. In junior high, high school, or college were the girls who fit into this category really respected? I'm sure they were popular and pursued by many boys *and* girls. But was that out of respect and true love, or out of lust and envy? Did her fans and male suitors care about her deepest desires and aspirations? Were they drawn to her character and enthralled by her talents, or just obsessed with the look of her face and body? That kind of lustful and envious attention lacks spiritual, emotional, and often physical fulfillment. I would bet at some point in that girl's life, she grew tired of people being nice to her just because she was pretty, and that she often wished for friends who loved her for herself. She imagined friends who would enjoy being around her because she was insightful, funny, or kind. She hoped someone would love her heart and not just her looks.

If you resemble the woman described above, please know I am not trying to offend you. In fact, I know outward beauty comes in all shades, sizes, and shapes. I most certainly do not fit the look described above, and yet I have always felt beautiful. I feel grateful not to have bought into the world's concept of beauty to the point of not feeling beautiful. And yet, I know growing up I did not understand real beauty…godly beauty.

As a young girl, I was popular and often pursued by boys because I was considered cute. And at that time, I used my popularity with boys to what I thought was *my advantage*. As it turns out, much of the favor I sought and received from boys was cheap, shallow, futile, and sinful. I used my body to get what I wanted. And although I was an "A" student, played sports, and was never caught for my criminal activities, my relationships were focused around sex and flirtatious behavior. Sure the boys got what they wanted, but at the time I thought I was getting what I wanted, too. I never felt used. In fact, I often felt like I was in control of those relationships.

I did have a type of confidence about me that others seemed drawn to. I felt in control, yet I was deceived. I was a slave to Satan even though I felt successful and powerful. My behavior was selfish, prideful, and immoral. That type of behavior led to the demise of my character. I might have been cute, but my heart and my actions were ugly. My mom would always say to me, "God don't like ugly." I would refrain from responding out loud, but I was thinking, "I'm not ugly, so you must be confused." Of course my mother was right. And it wasn't until I was much older that I began to understand what she meant by *ugly*. When you compromise your morals and body, your mind and attitude will follow.

By the time I was nineteen, I was bitter, arrogant, self-deceived, and self-righteous. I had little or no respect for men. It was my boyfriend, who later became my husband, that pointed out to me that I was foul, mean, and difficult to love. He didn't usually use those words, but he was trying to tell me I needed to change. Unfortunately, I missed much of his point, just as I had missed my mother's point years before.

Looking back now, that confidence I had was 50% a love for me no matter what, and a strong belief in my ability to achieve whatever I set out to do. The other 50% was arrogance, pride, and self-righteousness, mixed with much self-deception. It was worldly confidence. All these years I've thought it was a good thing. And in many ways that first 50% has helped me achieve many wonderful things and not let other people define who I am. And yet my behavior is still too often ugly.

I know God made me a confident person. I'm certain of it. Yet God's view of confidence is very different than the one I grew up with and still have in some ways. I grew up believing being submissive was a sign of weakness. I also have a desire to be heard, so having a quiet spirit is difficult for me to embrace. Yet these are the principles of God:

> Your beauty should not come from outward adornment, such as braided hair and the wearing of gold jewelry and fine clothes. Instead, it should be that of your inner self, the unfading beauty of a gentle and quiet spirit, which is of great worth in God's sight. For this is the way the holy women of the past who put their hope in God used to make themselves beautiful. They were submissive to their own husbands, like Sarah, who obeyed Abraham and called him her master. You are her daughters if you do what is right and do not give way to fear.
>
> (1 Pet. 3:3-6)

Wow! I've been a Christian for thirteen years and that scripture still challenges me. I'm OK with the part about your beauty should come from your inner spirit and not outward adornment. I get stuck on the "gentle and quiet spirit" part. If God had only said a bold and determined spirit, I could relate to that. Naturally, I portray those characteristics. But gentle and quiet is hard for me to wrap my mind around. What does God mean by gentle and quiet? Does he mean being passive and saying nothing when you want to speak, letting others walk all over you? I have to be honest. Unpleasant images of a human wallflower and pansy come to mind. That is Satan filling my head with lies.

God is not trying to discourage me or you when he says to be gentle and quiet. In fact, his image of a beautiful woman is meant to encourage and guide you. When God says gentle he means to not be aggressive, harsh, or mean spirited. He doesn't mean passive, or lacking confidence, or allowing people to walk all over you. The Lord wants you to embrace patience and love as you deal with every situation.

Quiet in God's dictionary is not about volume as much as it is about presence and presentation. Surely, the Father doesn't want you yelling and screaming all day long. However, what he means by a quiet spirit is one that is not overbearing or intimidated. Usually low self-esteem, fear, or sin causes you to act in ways that are harried, anxious, or timid.

I can be intimidating, and gentle is a characteristic I have to mediate on daily to achieve regularly. So I know I need God, because scaring others with my presence, tongue, or actions is not loving and humble. As well, the Lord doesn't want you to live your life afraid to experience his blessings or stand up for your convictions.

God is discipling my heart as I write this chapter. He is showing me my nature is still too worldly. Remember, in the Introduction of this book, I mentioned that if you want to master something you have to teach it. Well, I am teaching you about the beauty and usefulness of a gentle and quiet spirit because I am working to master this principle of God.

The Father made woman to be fearfully made. Others are to stand in awe of woman, not be fearful of her. There is a difference. Standing in awe means to be wowed by your majestic inner beauty and lifted up for the place you hold in the family as a woman: the bearer of life, the nurturer of the family, and as one responsible for shepherding the heart of God in others.

To be fearful of woman because she has become bitter, angry, and intimidating is not God's image of woman. The world praises women for being mean, demanding, and snotty. I refuse to repeat the word that is used for this kind of woman. It's on key chains, t-shirts, license plates, and now spoken freely on television and radio stations, and in songs and movies. The world has a much distorted view of womanly beauty and power. I am grateful for the Lord's definition of beautiful. It is what I'd rather be striving for and not pursuing Satan's definition.

You must embrace your glorious inner strength if you want to be and feel beautiful. Remember that you have God's character woven into the depths of your heart. He would never expect something from you or me that we cannot achieve; because nothing is impossible for the woman who puts her trust in the Lord. You don't have to worry about being taken advantage of or being walked all over. You can hold your tongue when necessary and select a more appropriate time to speak the truth in love (Eph. 4:15) as a gentle and quiet woman of God. Let your confidence in the Lord *be* your confidence.

You have many examples of obedient and spiritually powerful women in the Bible to follow. Your *Divine Sister,* the Sinful Woman, who gently and quietly washed Jesus' feet, is your example. You can embrace gentleness, like she did, as a portrayal of love, patience, and humility, not being pushy or mean-spirited. You can embrace quietness, like she did, refraining from the obvious of yelling and screaming, but more so having a spirit that is not afraid, frazzled, or anxious, because you trust in the Lord wholeheartedly.

Know that apart from the Lord and his *divine* ways, you are ugly. So grab hold of the Father and your glorious inner strength will empower you to overcome every obstacle you encounter. You'll become radiant and extraordinary, determined to successfully cross your finish line in the spiritual race to live eternally with Jesus in heaven.

If you are like me and struggle with having a gentle and quiet spirit which is of great worth in the eyes of the Lord, or your struggle is being a people pleaser or a loner, I hope you will cling to the Lord and allow him to massage your heart to experience the glory and freedom in building up your inner strength.

I feel like a weight has been lifted from me because another of God's mysteries has become clearer to me. And even though I am a masterpiece, I am also a work in progress, able to improve with each passing day. I suddenly have an image of Beauty and the Beast from the Disney movie. Yet, instead of their being two individual characters, Beauty and the Beast are one creature. That is not a pretty image. If you have been the Beast with behavior that is sinful and ugly, you can stop. The Father is waiting to forgive you. You can overcome the Beast in you with the Beauty of the Lord that is waiting to be released in full measure within you.

As a sinner, there will always be something in your character with which you struggle, there to remind you of why you need God's grace and mercy. Yet Scriptures also remind you that godly beauty has been achieved before. Sarah was recognized as beautiful in the eyes of the Lord and her husband (1 Pet. 3:5-6). Obviously Jesus' mother, Mary, was beautiful to God. She possessed that glorious inner strength God adores, so much so that she was chosen above all other women to bear the Son of God. Then there was the Sinful Woman and the Woman Who Bled who overcame their situations to embrace God. Queen Esther is another one of your *Divine Sisters* in the Bible whose beauty can be seen in her reverence for the Lord, submission to her husband, and courage to speak up for her people. Read the entire book of Esther to learn more about Queen Vashti and Queen Esther.

Read Their Story

The book of Esther shows us glorious inner beauty in action. Let's compare Queen Vashti to Queen Esther. Vashti, Esther's predecessor, was beautiful. She appeared confident as she entertained the women in the royal palace during the banquet King Xerxes was hosting. However, Vashti was arrogant and refused to come to her husband when he requested her. She was disrespectful and embarrassed the king in front of his guests. Although she had outer beauty Vashti did not allow her glorious inner beauty to shine through. The king and his advisors decided the queen's behavior had to be dealt with harshly because she was a role model for all the other women in the kingdom. They feared "there [would] be no end of disrespect and discord" (Esther 1:18) if the queen's conduct was allowed to go unpunished. So Vashti was removed from the throne for her ugly behavior.

On the other hand Esther was a young virgin, lovely in form and features (Est. 2:7), and she won the favor of everyone around her, including King Xerxes. However, she eventually used her high position, inner spirit, and faith in the Lord to help her save her people from annihilation. The difference between Vashti and Esther was their power source.

When Esther was tested she turned to her power source, the Lord, for strength and courage. As a gentle and quiet spirit she did not shrink back from the challenge. Instead she embraced the spirit of God within her and prepared her heart for the task before her. Esther fasted for three days with her people, during which time she prepared her heart and mind to go before the king. She knew she could die, yet she was willing to sacrifice herself to help others.

Esther remained humble and quiet as she boldly stood in front of the king's hall so he would notice her and grant her permission to come into his presence and speak. It may seem odd that the queen would have to wait to be summoned to speak to the king, her husband, but that was not Esther's battle to fight. She submitted to her husband's rule, trusting that the Lord would provide a way for her to be heard. Esther could have barged into the king's chambers. She could have spoken forcefully, demanding the king listen to her and give her what she wanted. Instead, when the king acknowledged her, she chose to serve him for two whole days before she addressed her urgent concern with him. Her patience and humility are impressive and worthy of imitation.

In comparison, Vashti relied on herself. She angrily denied her husband. I imagine Vashti knew the king and his friends would be drunk and was disgusted by their debauchery, and even afraid of what they might do to her if she appeared before them. What woman would want to go to them? She did not want to be paraded through his party as a trophy. She wanted respect and love, so she demanded it. She allowed fear to guide her and not God. Vashti handled herself in a very disrespectful and arrogant manner and her behavior resulted in being dismissed as the queen. Her plan backfired.

> There is a way that seems right to a [wo]man, but in the end it leads to death.
>
> (Prov. 14:12)

Vashti's way led to her demise. If she had trusted in the Lord she would have found a way to graciously and forgivingly respond to her husband. Vashti could have sent the eunuch back to King Xerxes with a message expressing her desire to please him, yet afraid of being defiled by the drunkenness of the king's guests. Although Vashti may have been able to discern the type of environment she would have been walking into, as a wife and queen she had an obligation to respond to her husband, the king, with respect and love. Vashti chose her way over the way of the Lord.

In difficult situations similar to Vashti's, God calls you to imitate Jesus. When you draw on your glorious inner strength you are able to make decisions that honor the Lord, yourself, and those around you. Esther made the right choice and is forever remembered as the queen who saved her people with her faith, humility, and inner beauty.

Has your way, which you initially thought was right, ever led to self-inflicted pain and turmoil? Vashti provides a great lesson in what not to do and how pride is the downfall of woman. I know I have behaved like Vashti on too many occasions. In addition, over the years I have mistaken my pride and arrogance as confidence. In those moments, I did not rely on God. I relied on myself.

Learn from Vashti and Esther: real beauty is internal and illuminated by following the principles of God. When you do not follow God, that is when you are really ugly and have a false sense of beauty. You do not shine or sparkle, though you were created with radiance. Darkness covers your spirit so "the light" placed in your soul cannot be seen. Therefore, your attractiveness to yourself and others is diminished.

You must ask yourself, are you tapping into the right power source? The right power source is from God. His power is always available, never-ending, strong, fervent, reliable, and provides you with the ideal nourishment to feed your mind, body, and heart. When you tap into Christ's strength and courage you become powerful beyond measure.

The wrong source has little or no power, providing you with no strength to keep on going or to make the changes in your life that you know you need to. Sometimes the wrong power source has only temporary power, allowing you to feel temporary happiness and taste fleeting success. This leads to frustration and confusion. You can feel some success, but you cannot sustain it. The reason you cannot sustain happiness, or peace, or joy is because you are relying on yourself or another human being and not relying on the Creator of the Universe.

When a woman fails to depend on God's power, her life is consumed with frustration, anxiety, anger, worry, fear, lethargy, a sense of powerlessness, and mediocrity. She feels hopeless; on many days it's a struggle to just exist. Her life is void of true joy and love. Some women never see their desperation, yet they act in very desperate ways: vying for power and money, sleeping around, getting drunk, taking risks with their lives; compromising their bodies, ideals, values, minds, and dreams because they stop believing in themselves, or they have a misguided perspective of love and happiness.

Other women are so angry that they push their family and friends away; they drink, curse, yell, hit, and use words like daggers to force others to do what they want. They mask their fear with bitterness and superiority. They are mean-spirited and use every disappointment to cut people down to size with their vicious tongues. And then there are women who have lost their voice and never speak up for themselves. They hold their heads down, hearts dragging on the ground, tired, anxious, and too afraid to move. They stay in their small worlds because they are sickly comfortable living in fear. All these women are painful pictures of the walking dead. They have given up their natural and pure power simply by not recognizing it.

Which woman are you? Are you sick and tired of feeling powerless? Of course you are. So stop it! Tap into the Lord's power, one simple action at a time, one decision at a time.

The Greatest Miracle in the World written by Og Mandino states that the greatest miracle is for a (woman) to return from the living dead and embrace the power God has given to (her) to change the path of (her) desperate life. Each (woman) has this power within (her). You have been given this power from God. Tapping into God's powerhouse will give you that confidence and strength you require to overcome all the challenges in your life: low self-esteem, depression, illness, marital strife, anger, death of a loved one, loneliness, financial problems; you name it, God can conquer it.

> Trust God from the bottom of your heart; don't try to figure everything out on your own. Listen for God's voice in everything you do, everywhere you go; he's the one who will keep you on track.
>
> (Prov. 3:5-6, THE MESSAGE)

Stop fighting the Lord and cling to him because your life, salvation, and peace of mind depend on God. A transformation of your heart, mind, and life will occur if you take the leap of faith to follow Jesus. The Lord is waiting for you to come to him with an open heart ready to receive true, unconditional love and ready to *really* do it his way; not try it, but DO it. Nike's slogan, "Just do it," really says, "Stop playing games and get to it, already!"

However, God is not someone you can visit once in a while and feel completely connected with. You have to stay and live with him, enjoying his shelter, learning from his teachings, and daily applying his principles to your life. Going to church twice a year on Easter or Christmas does not constitute being plugged in or being a Christian. A true relationship with Christ requires a permanent and daily connection. Just like being married, a husband and wife must connect daily, constantly thinking through the needs, desires, and expectations of the other to have a marriage that will grow and flourish. A powerful relationship with the Father requires daily devotion and attention to change your life and positively influence the lives of those around you.

> Watch your life and doctrine closely. Persevere in them, because if you do, you will save both yourself and your hearers.
>
> (1 Tim. 4:16)

Now is the time to arm yourself with true love, a right self-image, and godly confidence. The right kind of love is God's love. Embracing God's love provides you with the truth of who you are and who you were created to be. A right self-image is that of a valuable and loved daughter of The King—talented, gifted, and chosen to be an ambassador for Christ (2 Cor. 5:20). If you really want to be beautiful, tap into the power of God. Outward beauty is fleeting and your inner beauty is the only type of beauty that will last. It is amazing to me that more people aren't running towards God. Our world is so image and beauty conscious, you would think by now more people would have picked up on the certain fact that eternal beauty lies with God. It is amazing how Satan has deceived the world into believing the next fashion trend, or expensive purchase, or fad diet, or surgery will make you more beautiful and make you love yourself more.

God is where your positive self-esteem and self-worth come from. Others…men…cannot give that to you. People can nurture your self-esteem or help to destroy it. You allow either one. However, loving yourself is a gift, an inheritance given to you by God. The Lord does warn you to think of yourself with sober judgment, not thinking more highly of yourself than you ought to (Rom. 12:3). Notice the Lord does not say you should not think highly of yourself at all. He cautions against thinking <u>too</u> much of yourself to the point of being arrogant and snotty.

Remember the opening scripture, Psalm 139:14, "I praise you because I am fearfully and wonderfully made; your works are wonderful, I know that full well." Notice the scripture is a bold affirmation of godly confidence. It attests to being wonderful, worthy of awe, and knowing full well that everything the Lord creates is magnificent.

That scripture has absolutely no elements of timidity or shame, because you are amazing!

Have you stopped believing in your splendor? Have you lost your certainty of how fabulous the Lord made you? When you tap into God's love, it will rejuvenate that inner beauty and godly confidence that says, "I am worthy. I am beautiful because I am the magnum opus of the Lord. I have his *divine* character and wonderful talents." (Write that bold affirmation down, post in on your bathroom mirror, and repeat it to yourself five times a day…forever!) Measure yourself by the Lord's standards so you will have godly confidence in yourself and your position as daughter to The King.

Be confident. Know that the Lord sees your beauty. God is saying to you, "Love yourself now, because I love you. Focus on developing your godly character; then your inner beauty and strength will brilliantly shine through."

Tap into God's power and visualize his perfect image of you. Accept his restoring and unconditional love, because greatness in every measure awaits you. All you have to do is embrace your *divinity* as a daughter of The King.

DEEPEN YOUR PERSONAL CONVICTIONS

READ: Esther 4:12-16; 1 Peter 3:3-5; Ephesians 3:16-21

1. How are you tapping into God's power?

2. What happens when you rely on your own power and strength?

3. In what ways (silently or boisterously) do you claim to be stronger than the Lord?

4. What can you learn from Queen Esther about having a gentle and quiet spirit?

5. Pray daily to put aside your pride and desire to do things your way. Then pray some more to become the gentle and quiet woman of God you were created to be.

CHAPTER 10
Embracing Your Divinity Part 1

Commit everything you do to the LORD. Trust him, and he will help you.

(Ps. 37:5, NLT)

Now that you know you are *wonderfully made* by the hand of God, and created to live a *divine* and purposeful life, what should you do? Should you run out and get baptized? Should you drag your neighbor into your home and force them to follow Jesus? Maybe you should fall to your knees and pray for the Lord to *deliver you*.

Although I'm being facetious (it was time for some comic relief), that last idea might prove very fruitful if done with sincerity. I believe this book is some of the fruit you desire. Certainly, I cannot claim you are destined to be a *Divine Princess* and then leave you with no practicals on how to embrace your *divinity* and honor God with your life.

So hang on, this chapter and the next may seem simple, yet they are powerful, and will change your life if you follow this advice with an open and teachable heart.

Seek God with All Your Heart, Soul, and Mind

Remember, when you wholeheartedly seek the Lord you will not be disappointed.

Seeking God requires sincerity to be open and true as you call upon the Lord and ask for his help. You are not doing it to impress others, or just to save your skin, or to support some misguided desire. You sincerely believe it is Jesus' help you need.

> All a [wo]man's ways seem innocent to [her], but motives are weighed by the Lord.
>
> (Prov. 16:2)

Seeking God requires humility to recognize your weaknesses and admit your daily need for God. (However, being humble does not require you to focus on your faults to the point of tearing down your self-esteem.) Humility also allows you to call on your spiritual friend and ask for help or to say, "I'm sorry," when you know you are wrong.

> Humble yourselves before the Lord, and he will lift you up.
>
> (James 4:10)

Seeking God requires honesty to truly share your heart with the Lord and tell him what is really going on with you. Not that the Lord doesn't already know, but because he wants you to be honest with him and with yourself. Everything is not always OK or fine. Sometimes, maybe often, your situation is terrible or at least less than desirable.

In addition, self-deceit is destructive and will continue to hurl you down the wrong path until disaster strikes and knocks you off your lying horse.

> The LORD detests lying lips, but he delights in [wo]men who are truthful.
>
> (Prov. 12:22)

Seeking God requires action making it necessary for you to take specific steps to find God. Daily you have to pray, study the Scriptures, repent of your sin, and be open about your needs in order to find God.

> You see that [her] faith and [her] actions were working together, and [her] faith was made complete by what [she] did.
>
> (James 2:22)

Pray: Ask God for Help

Ask God to help you through your situation. He hears those who pray to him earnestly and with the right motives. Tell him what you need and desire. Don't be silent about what you want to see happen. Be very specific and share with God the detail of your situation and the detail of the outcome you envision.

In September 1995, one month after Darryl and I celebrated our first wedding anniversary, Darryl asked me for a divorce. At that time, we were not Christians and we were not living the way God wanted us to.

I have to admit that my first response was shock, then fear, then anger. As a prideful and independent woman, who has always thought highly of herself, I told Darryl to go. "If you don't want to be with me, I don't want to be with you." That statement was both a lie and the truth. I didn't want to be with someone who didn't want me, and yet I knew I was in love and didn't want him to leave. But I didn't know how to fix us or me, so I let my pride respond to Darryl. On the outside, I acted with bravado, as if I didn't need anyone. On the inside, I was anxious with fear, sadness, and anger. I feared no other man would want to be with a woman who already had a child. I imagined a lonely future riddled with bitterness. I was angry with myself for not being able to control my attitude or be humble.

One of the reasons Darryl wanted a divorce was because I was so disrespectful to him. My husband is a calm and, at that time, a more passive man. (God has changed him, too!) He expressed to me that he loved me, but he didn't like me and just couldn't deal with me. He wanted to end our relationship before he began to hate me.

One day when I was home alone, I fell to my knees in prayer. I cried so hard, my chest hurt and I gasped for each breath. I poured out my heart to God and begged him to help me. I knew I could change for a little while on my own, but I could not manifest long term change. I needed God to save my marriage, to keep me from being bitter, and to continue to love my eighteen month old daughter well.

> Don't fret or worry. Instead of worrying, pray. Let petitions and praises shape your worries into prayers, letting God know your concerns. Before you know it, a sense of God's wholeness, everything coming together for good, will come and settle you down. It's wonderful what happens when Christ displaces worry at the center of your life.
>
> (Phil. 4:6-7, THE MESSAGE)

I prayed for weeks and months. The situation with Darryl remained the same. He wanted a divorce and I refused to show him the extent of my heartache and vulnerability.

My heart softened enough to be open before God, yet not open with Darryl. God is faithful and rescues those who call on him. In December that year, I met Alyssa, who became my friend. She was and still is spiritually wise and obedient to the Lord. She shared her life with me and showed me the Scriptures in new ways, helping me to understand better what I grew up reading in church and the religiously affiliated schools I attended.

Today, Darryl and I have been married for fourteen years. We are happy and in love. Of course, we are still sinners. However, now we know where to turn for answers and we continually rely upon God, the Bible, and our church family for guidance.

Go to Church

There are many churches in the world and more than 400 denominations worldwide, so how do you pick a church? Church is not meant to be like Burger King—any way you want it. God's church honestly and completely obeys his doctrine as written in the Scriptures and not the made up doctrine of (a) man. A Bible-based church *holds each member accountable* for living like Jesus daily, not just on Sundays.

The purpose of going to church is to worship and praise God. The benefits of Christian fellowship: encouragement and serving others also come from going to church. Individually and collectively the church is commissioned to help others know the Word of God (Matt. 28:18-20).

In the book of Acts, Paul describes the devotion of the brothers and sisters in the church.

> They devoted themselves to the apostles' teaching and to the fellowship, to the breaking of bread and to prayer. Everyone was filled with awe, and many wonders and miraculous signs were done by the apostles. All the believers were together and had everything in common. Selling their possessions and goods, they gave to anyone as he had need. Every day they continued to meet together in the temple courts. They broke bread in their homes and ate together with glad and sincere hearts, praising God and enjoying the favor of all the people. And the Lord added to their number daily those who were being saved.
>
> (Acts 2:42-47)

Keep in mind the church is not the building. The church is the people of the Lord, devoted and obedient to Christ, and loving towards people in and out of the church. The Father notices when you are missing, because you are meant to fulfill a meaningful role in the family of God. Your role is determined by your heart and the gifts and talents God has given to you. There are no small or irrelevant roles. Each role is significant to the Lord and important for the family of God to function as he intended (1 Cor. 12:12-26).

Hebrew 10:25, warns us "not to give up meeting together, as some are in the habit of doing." This means that television church alone does not honor God, nor does it have the feel of devotion or family like in Acts 2 and 1 Corinthians 12. You cannot build relationships and enjoy the fellowship of your spiritual brothers and sisters by watching church services on TV or listening to services on the radio. There is no real action in sitting on your couch listening to someone, no matter how righteous or spiritual the speaker may appear. Even reading this book is not enough to be right with God. *You have to act.* One action that will please the Lord is attending church weekly and getting involved in church activities.

If you are disabled, ill, or house bound, TV or radio services are only one way to praise and worship God. Ask your minister or spiritually wise friend to visit with you and have worship service at your home with a few people (Matt. 18:20). Pray with someone over the phone. Send a card of encouragement to a brother or sister in need. Employ your creativity and search for ways to honor and serve God even though your situation may be limiting.

> Jesus replied: "Love the Lord your God with all your heart and with all your soul and with all your mind." This is the first and greatest commandment. And the second is like it: "Love your neighbor as yourself."

> All the Law of the Prophets hang on these two commandments.
>
> (Matt. 22:37-40)

These commandments are intertwined. You must love God wholeheartedly in order to love your neighbor deeply. Likewise, if you don't love your neighbor, you cannot truly love God (1 John 4:20-21). In fact, true love for Christ compels you to act out your faith with love and in service to others.

So many women have said to me, "I don't need to go to church because my relationship with God is private or I don't like organized religion." Yes, it is important for you to spend time alone with God, but he never intended for you to worship alone all the time. Jesus sought time alone with God, yet he was usually surrounded by many people whom he worshipped with daily. In addition, the church requires organization; without it there would be chaos, misinterpretation of the Scriptures, a lack of accountability for living like Jesus, and God would not be glorified.

The church is made up of God's children, his family. He gave us to each other as a gift to be cherished and appreciated. He expects his family to worship together, to love and nurture one another, to strengthen and serve one another, and to encourage and hold one another accountable for living a righteous life. There are many appropriate times in your life when you need to be alone with God. However, a family cannot grow in their love and devotion to one another if they are never together and don't share their lives with each other.

> Let us not become weary in doing good, for at the proper time we will reap a harvest if we do not give up. Therefore, as we have opportunity, let us do good

> to all people, especially to those who belong to the family of believers.
>
> (Gal. 6:9-10)

As a woman you love the concept of unity, of getting along and working together. You would never expect a loving family to say to each member, "I don't need you. I don't want you in my life. I can exist alone." With that said, if you are not an active member of a church right now, the time has come to obey God on this command.

Characteristics to Look for in a Church Home

1. The Bible is taught in its entirety in worship services and in Bible studies. No one is adding to or taking away from the Word. Every page of the Bible is taught. No page or Scripture is omitted because it is difficult to obey or hard to hear.
2. Each church member, even the ministry staff, is held accountable to live like Jesus daily through a personal relationship with God. Each member is called to love God up close and personal. A personal relationship with the Lord is deep, meaningful, and causes you to act out your love and faith. However, just going to church or even praying regularly does not mean you have a deep and personal relationship with God. The affect Jesus' sacrifice and the Word have on your heart is an indication of how deep your relationship with God is.
3. Each church member, even the ministry staff, has one or several spiritual advisors who help him/her obey the Scriptures and grow and develop in his/her character and spiritual maturity. The Bible calls you to seek advice in every area of your life: relationships, marriage, parenting, marital

intimacy, finances, work, service, education, etc. No area of your life is off limits.

4. Each church member is reaching out to those who don't know Jesus, helping others understand how to have a personal and deep relationship with the Lord. Everyone (not just the ministry staff) is commissioned by Jesus to spread the Word of the Gospel everywhere they go (Matt. 28:18-20).
5. There is unity and a sincere love and devotion to one another and the different ministries in the church (youth, singles, marrieds, seniors, music, community outreach, etc.). In numerous Scriptures throughout the Bible you are commanded to obey your leaders (Heb. 13:17) and make every effort to be unified to the body of Christ (Eph. 4:2-6).

I have been at my church for more than twelve years. The first time I went, I recognized something different than the other churches I had attended. I recognized love and sincerity for everyone, even new people. As I got to know several members of the church, they shared their lives with me and were genuinely interested in helping me have a devoted and loving relationship with God. They helped me to study and understand the Scriptures in ways I had never done before, even though I had grown up in religious environments.

I am fortunate to belong to a Bible-based church that holds each member accountable for how he/she is living daily. I have several spiritual advisors whom I turn to regularly for spiritual guidance on every aspect of my life.

If you live in the Las Vegas, Nevada area, I highly recommend my church, the Greater Las Vegas Church of Christ. If you live in another city, we have sister churches all over the world. At the end of this book you will find the website of my church. You will also find a website which will help you locate our sister churches around the world.

With that said, know that any church you attend has flaws. A long time ago, Margaret Hodge, one of my Women's Ministry Leaders, told me that "the church is perfect, but the people are not." So do not expect perfection. Yet, for members and ministry staff alike, there must be a sincere and daily devotion to God; love for all; personal and group accountability to follow the Scriptures; humble and diligent repentance; grace and forgiveness; and a continual reaching out to others.

Find a SWOF

A what? A *SWOF*! A Spiritually Wise and Obedient Friend. I could simply say seek the advice of a friend. But you don't really want advice from just anybody. You, a woman wholeheartedly seeking God, want the advice of a woman (or man) who truly loves the Lord. The life of your *SWOF* clearly demonstrates her love for Christ through her spiritual wisdom, deep convictions, and obedience to the Scriptures. The Bible calls you "a fool" for not listening to advice (Prov. 12:15). Yet you are considered wise and your plans will succeed when you seek advice (Prov. 15:22).

This may hurt when you read this, but some of your friends may be playing Christian. They may know the Scriptures and can repeat them at will, however they are not living out the Scriptures. They may go to church regularly, yet complain about everything that has to do with church, like serving others, going to midweek services, giving contribution, and following every command (especially the challenging ones). They compare themselves to others, being critical of the church leadership, cursing, or my personal favorite—quick to share everything they just heard about someone, also known as gossip. Right now that woman is not the best choice for your *SWOF*.

Instead, choose a woman striving to be like Jesus. She is flawed, yet growing and learning from her mistakes, and willing to listen and advise without judgment. Pray for God to place her in your immediate path and for you to recognize her. It is likely she is praying to find you, too.

Study the Scriptures

Acts 17:11-12 says the Bereans examined the Scriptures everyday to see if what Paul said was true. Just like the Bereans, you should be reading your Bible daily. As you seek God he helps you understand what's in the Scriptures so you can rightfully live them out and build deep convictions of your own.

The Bereans studied the Word so they would know the Scriptures for themselves and not just take the word of Paul, a man passing through town. The same is true for you and me. As a woman who is seeking a personal relationship with God, you cannot live on the beliefs of your husband, parents, grandparents, ministers, or friends. You have to build up your own faith and convictions. And faith comes from hearing and reading the Word (Rom. 10:17).

In addition, the Bereans were recognized in the Bible as being of noble character because they diligently held to deep personal convictions. As you study the Bible, you will realize the Scriptures are living and active (Heb. 4:12-13), applicable to your life challenges. The Scriptures are also "useful for teaching, rebuking, correcting, and training in righteousness, so that [you] may be thoroughly equipped for every good work" (2 Tim. 3:16-17). Know that every word written in the Bible is from God. Although men are recognized as the writers of the books of the Bible, rest assured that those men were empowered by the Holy Spirit, and God used them as tools to get his words and commands on paper (2 Pet. 1:20-21).

Make the Bible Your Standard for Living

I grew up believing that the men who wrote the Bible wrote what they wanted to write, that there may not have always been *divine inspiration.* I would say that because I was ignorant, and had not read a lot of the Bible. I did not want to be confronted by the Scriptures and then be held accountable for my actions. Ultimately, I was rebellious, and did not want to change the way I was living.

I used to say that the Bible was written 2000 years ago, and was not relevant to what we experience today. I was dead wrong. *Dead wrong!* The Bible even addresses that attitude. God knew (wo)men would question its authenticity, authority, and righteousness.

Quite frankly, if men had written the Bible without God, then many of the commands that are in the Bible would have been omitted. You know…the Scriptures that tell you sex outside of marriage is a sin; lying is sinful even when others cannot tell you are lying; greed and the love of money are a form of idolatry; drunkenness is a sin; and homosexuality is completely against God (Eph. 5:3-5; Acts 5:1-10; Luke 16:13; 1 Tim. 6:10; Rom. 13:13-14; 1 Pet. 4:1-5). These and many more controversial subjects would go unaddressed or even be considered righteous if man alone had written the Bible.

I realize I may have just offended you. However, I did not write the Bible. I'm simply called to tell you accurately what it says, *without* deleting the hard to hear Scriptures that can be even more difficult to obey.

Divine Princesses are required to make the Bible their standard for living all of its pages, even the pages that may seem hurtful to some, insignificant, or too challenging to achieve.

Society would rather you live by watered down principles, allowing anything and everything into your life, mind, and body. God says otherwise. The Bible is your instruction manual for life. Your standard has to be God's Word, not man's word; not even your own word.

I have to admit, I have often been challenged by that part about the standard for my life cannot even be "my own word" (mostly because my sinful nature is also a control freak). However, I know for a certainty that as I embrace the Lord's Word and put it into practice, I can see the blessings in my life. Often my first instinct, usually guided by my emotions, is wrong. As I see the Word working in my life, I am reminded that the Lord is powerful and his way is always right. So be like Peter and the other disciples who replied: "We must obey God rather than men!" (Acts 5:29).

The Father calls for complete obedience to him.

> Do not let this Book of the Law depart from your mouth; meditate on it day and night, so that you may be careful to do everything written in it. Then you will be prosperous and successful.
>
> (Josh. 1:8)

The word "obedience" has taken on a very negative connotation in the world. Yet God loves this word, and as a woman I have grown to love and appreciate its meaning. Obedience to God and his Scriptures grants me forgiveness, salvation, freedom, protection, and prosperity for my life on earth and in heaven.

Obedience to God frees you from your slavery to sin, and allows you to enter God's Kingdom free of guilt, sorrow, and shame—and destined to live a blessed life on earth and eternally in heaven.

Confess Your Sins

As you read the Word, you become more familiar with what God describes as sin. There are several places in the Bible that list sins, including Galatians 5:19-21 and Proverbs 6:16-19. Read these Scriptures so you are equipped with the right information about sins and you understand that by which God will measure your life. Don't do like I did for years and avoid examining the Scriptures, hoping ignorance will save you. It surely will not!

I grew up going to religious schools, and in high school I started attending a Baptist church with a former boyfriend. So I had read a little bit of the Bible. I knew some of the miracles Jesus performed and a few of the stories in Scripture. However, I grew up believing that the stories in the Bible were just tales and not necessarily meant to be used as a guide for living, so I never really took the lessons seriously. I even got baptized at fifteen, yet I really did not understand the purpose for baptism and what it really meant. I did not build my own deep convictions about God or sin. I was doing all kinds of sinful things and really didn't understand the extent of my sin until I studied the Bible in January 1996.

As an adult woman, I was better able to understand what the Lord was saying. At that time, I was eager to receive God's help because my marriage was falling apart. In addition, I had several women help me and then hold me accountable for how I was living and behaving. They helped me understand repentance and godly sorrow as described in 2 Corinthians 7:10-11.

Repentance means to make a 180 degree turn away from sin. It requires action and humility to admit fault and take responsibility for the outcome, as well as seek guidance on how not to fall into that same sin again.

God also calls you to confess your sins to him and others (your *SWOF*) in order to receive healing. Confession requires openness and displays your humility before God. The Bible teaches you to confess your sins to another Christian woman (or man) so you can be prayed for and healed (James 5:16).

Once again, the reason I advise you to find a *SWOF* is because you want to confess your sins to someone who will listen without judgment, pray for and with you, give you spiritually wise guidance, and then hold you accountable for changing. At times you may have shared your sins with someone, even someone you trusted, but did they hold you accountable for changing? Repentance is evident by your actions (Acts 26:20). Without change you have not repented. And change is hard to maintain on your own. When you rely on your relationship with the Lord, the Word and your *SWOFs* will help you manifest long term change.

Get Baptized

Baptism is a controversial and misunderstood command of God. Baptism is more than an outward sign of an inward grace. It is required for forgiveness and it washes away your sins. Baptism works with the sacrifice of Jesus on the cross for you to have forgiveness and salvation. Baptism connects you to Jesus as it symbolizes his death, burial, and resurrection. Likewise, in baptism as you are fully submersed in water you experience the death and burial of your old self, your sins are washed away, and you are reborn to a new self.

In Acts 2:36-41 Peter warns everyone in the crowd to repent and get baptized for the forgiveness of their sins. The Bible says you cannot enter the kingdom of God without being born again of water and the Spirit (John 3:1-7). Even Jesus, who was without any personal sin and who possessed the unlimited power of God, was baptized (Luke 3:21-22). He submitted to the will of God because he recognized God as his Father and he wanted to do what was right in the eyes of the Lord (Matt. 3:13-17). And notice he was baptized as an adult, not as a child.

There are no examples of a baby or a child being baptized in the Bible. Becoming a Christian is a serious commitment—one to be made for a lifetime, like marriage. A person must be able to understand the commitment they are making to the Lord. Children are often unable to distinguish right from wrong, let alone make a lifetime commitment. I would never ask a twelve year old to get married, nor would I expect an infant to take on a husband and become his helper. Children are unable to comprehend the depth of being fully committed to the Lord for eternity. And this is a decision that should not be made by someone else for you.

Imitating Christ is your goal, and baptism *is* a command from God. Yes, baptism is a sign of obedience to God, not man. (I did not write that or any other command in the Bible).Without baptism you cannot have forgiveness from God and you cannot enter the kingdom of God. Without baptism you say Jesus' sacrifice on the cross was useless. His death allows you to be reborn…reborn a new creation (2 Cor. 5:17) through baptism and submission to

Christ. In baptism you follow Christ into the water to be cleansed of your sins and then you follow him in living out his principles and trusting in his plan for your life.

In addition, at baptism you receive the gift of the Holy Spirit as your wise Counselor (Titus 3:4-7). The Holy Spirit is given to you to provide you with counsel (John 14:26), and a clear conscious to make godly choices and honor the Lord with your life.

When I joined my church in 1996, I was baptized *for real*. I did this because after studying the Bible in 1996, I realized the first time I was baptized I just got wet. I was fifteen years old and very little about my life changed before or after that baptism. I did not really understand what I was committing myself to and what would be expected of me from that point forward. I had no repentance, no confession of my sins, no Bible study, and no *SWOF*s. My minister and church just got me wet, then left me to figure out my Christianity on my own as an immature and confused teenager with raging hormones who was in self-denial about sin and completely self-absorbed.

In contrast, in 1996 I had several *SWOF*s guiding me through my Bible studies where I developed personal convictions about the Word and made the Bible the standard for living my life. I am grateful to those women who helped me, and forever grateful to God for giving me a second chance to be with him.

It has taken me many years to appreciate the aforementioned principles and embrace my *divinity*. My hope is that you can learn from my mistakes and take these steps to propel you forward in your Christian walk as a *woman, wonderfully made*.

Deepen Your Personal Convictions

Read: Romans 12:1-2; Acts 8:26-39

1. If you are not attending church, what is stopping you?

2. How have you made the Bible your standard for living your life?

3. Who is your *SWOF*? Why did you choose her?

4. Are you willing to do whatever it takes to follow the Lord?

5. Pray daily for deep convictions about what the Bible says and to follow the Bible and not the ways and traditions of man.

CHAPTER 11

Embracing Your Divinity Part 2

And we pray this in order that you may live a life worthy of the Lord and may please him in every way: bearing fruit in every good work, growing in the knowledge of God, being strengthened with all power according to his glorious might so that you may have great endurance and patience, and joyfully giving thanks to the Father, who has qualified you to share in the inheritance of the saints in the kingdom of light.

(Col. 1:10-12)

In the previous chapter you learned you had to seek God with all your heart, soul, and mind. In seeking the Father you have to be honest, sincere, and humble. Prayer, going to church, and studying the Bible are crucial to connecting with God. In addition, you need a Spiritually Wise and Obedient Friend to whom you will confess your sins. Your *SWOF* will help you understand the Scriptures better and guide you through the process of being a Christian, someone who loves and obeys God wholeheartedly and continually. As you confess your sins and get baptized, you are reconciled to God's family. You no longer have to walk alone. You can experience the love and joy of being with your spiritual family in your Father's home.

Once you have accepted Christ as your Savior, the work begins for living as a Christian. Embracing your *divinity* requires you to live like Jesus everyday. I know that may sound difficult and intimidating, yet as you train yourself to be like Jesus you'll experience many days where embracing your *divinity* seems easy and you experience few challenges. Then there are those days when you'll look in the mirror and *divine* is not what you see or feel. You feel like another "d" word: the devil, damned, doomed, desperate, desolate, dangerous, deprived, and dogged by everyone and everything.

It is possible to be *divine* and not feel *divine* or behave *divinely*. However, God always sees you as *divine*. To him, you are always his beautiful creation: cherished, loved, and desired. There isn't a moment that goes by that he doesn't want to be with you. You are a sinner—he knows this. Yet he also knows that with him your life is powerful, fruitful, and majestic.

So how do you continue to embrace God so you can be powerful beyond imagination? Pay attention and put these principles into practice.

Obey God in Every Aspect of Your Life

God placed you on this earth for a reason. He wants you to know true love—pure, deep, unconditional, tangible, and fulfilling. He wants you to share that love with others. He wants you to have life to the fullest. He wants you to have the desires of your heart. He has more blessings in store for you than you can count or imagine. "What are they?" you ask. "Where are they?"

The Lord has one condition—only one—obey him in every aspect of your life. Obedience is a word that is misunderstood in many cultures today. Adults expect obedience from children, yet adults despise the concept of being obedient. Once we become adults we instantly rebel and the word obedience is no longer a part of our vocabulary, except when it comes to our children. The Lord expects obedience. The Lord blesses obedience. And obedience to the Lord produces fruit beyond what you can imagine.

> And this is love: that we walk in obedience to his commands. As you have heard from the beginning, his command is that you walk in love."
>
> (2 John 1:6)

You fool yourself if you claim to love God, but do not obey him. In order to be a Christian you have to be obedient to God's Word. There is no way around this. He calls you to obey the Scriptures in every aspect of your life. Are you willing to turn your life over to God and follow his plan for your life?

Grow and Mature in the Lord

As a woman seeking the heart of God it is your responsibility to mature in your Christianity. This is not the sole responsibility of your minister, nor the responsibility of your parents, husband, or friends. You are first and foremost responsible for your relationship with the Lord and securing your salvation.

God desires for your relationship with him to be personal and deep. Only you can make that happen. Everyday you must spend time with the Lord, reading your Bible, praying and sharing with him how your life is going, what you need, confessing your sin, and praying for others and for situations. This type of worship and reverence for the Lord fosters a deep relationship.

Maturity is also developed as you persevere through trials and struggles in your life.

> Suffering produces perseverance; perseverance, character; and character, hope.
>
> (Rom. 5:3-4)

In order for your character to mature you have to be challenged. If life were easy, then you would never mature in character, heart, or mind.

If you are feeling hopeless, know that any struggle you are experiencing is an opportunity for you to grow. You are allowed to experience challenges so that you will see your need for God and call on him to help you persevere. Remember, hope is produced when you persevere as a result of relying on the Lord to guide you through good and bad times.

Live a Pure and Holy Life

> Live a life worthy of the calling you have received.
>
> (Eph. 4:1)

As you continue to read the following Scriptures in Ephesians 4, the Father urges you to be completely humble, patient, forgiving, and unified to the Spirit. There is no tolerance for the old, ugly things you used to do. Jesus is not expecting perfection, however he does expect you to pursue purity and holiness. In today's world this can be extremely hard with sexual images, advertisements, and depictions of loose and provocative "fun" bombarding your mind, vision, and physical space. Jesus never intended for you to give your body, mind, and soul away to anyone but your husband; not even to someone who might become your husband one day.

> There must not be even a hint of sexual immorality, or of any kind of impurity, or of greed, because these are improper for God's holy people.
>
> (Eph. 5:3)

This must be one of the hardest principles for women to embrace. Yet God has a plan for your body. Your body is the Lord's temple. Remember, at baptism you receive the gift of the Holy Spirit. You sin against your own self, in addition to God, when you have sex outside of marriage. At the time of marriage, your body, your most intimate self is meant to be a gift to your husband. Until that time God expects you to live a celibate life. Yes, celibate. I did not misspell celebrate.

A true Christian church teaches its youth and single people to honor the Lord with their bodies as instruments of service through a love for Christ. A true Christian church will teach the meaning and purpose of leading a pure life. They will provide practical guidance for avoiding the temptations of this world that devalues God, women, purity, marriage, and the human body.

As a woman who did not live a pure life before marriage, I can tell you first hand that having sex outside of marriage scars you for life in ways that negatively affect your relationship with God and your husband. Aside from sexually transmitted diseases and unwanted pregnancies, once you have sex with someone you have bonded with that person in a way that was only intended for a husband and wife. Sex is meant to produce an intimate bond (and of course, children). Once you marry, old images of previous sexual partners can destroy or at least impede your intimacy with your husband (even the seemingly good images are bad). Comparisons of your husband to other men can create guilt, hostility, and bitterness in your relationship. God never intended that for you or your husband.

In addition, if you allow sex and flirtatious and seductive behavior into your relationship prior to marriage, you can create a superficial relationship that has no depth of friendship, unconditional love, deep respect, and real intimacy. Not to mention no foundation of Christ. Surely, the depth of every marriage is tested many times and if your relationship is founded in physical attraction, sexual promiscuity, and other forms of immorality, your relationship will fail over time, leaving you bitter, discouraged, and full of guilt and shame.

Please know that purity does not just deal with sexual behavior. Purity and holiness also mean avoiding drugs, drunkenness (even being tipsy), smoking, cursing, foul talk, coarse joking, greed, debauchery, idol worship (you can be the idol = selfishness), and anything that comes before the Lord. Review the sin lists mentioned in the previous chapter under the section labeled *Confess Your Sins*.

Please don't let the principle of purity discourage you; that would be Satan's desire. You know the sins mentioned above do not bring real happiness or true love. They mask what is really troubling you and they prevent you from understanding your true needs spiritually, emotional, and physically.

> There is a way that seems right to a [wo]man, but in the end it leads to death.
>
> (Prov. 14:12)

Don't let your selfish desires or the world's misguided representation of relationships and sex lead you to death. Know that the Lord's way is always right and he promises you a full and complete life if you follow his principles.

Help Others to Know Christ

After Jesus died and returned to the apostles, he left them with one last command before ascending into heaven.

> All authority in heaven and on earth has been given to me. Therefore go and make disciples of all nations, baptizing them in the name of the Father and of the Son and of the Holy Spirit, and teaching them to obey everything I have commanded you. And surely I am with you always, to the very end of the age.
>
> (Matt. 28:18-20)

This is known as The Great Commission. It is an expectation and command God has for every person walking the planet. Of course, only those who love and obey his commands take it to heart and make it their life purpose. As a *Divine Princess* this is your life mission—to help others know, love, and obey Jesus in a deep and personal way, using your talents and the many gifts the Father has given to you.

Once again, I know it sounds intimidating and may not even be what you thought you would be doing with your life. Yet if you truly embrace your *divinity* and acknowledge your place in God's family as the daughter of The King, you will understand your self-worth according to the Lord, who wants so intensely to be your Father. Then you will see how you can accomplish this mission set before you.

Use Your Talents to Please God

Please don't start reading this by telling yourself you don't have any talents. You do, and probably many talents. In Matthew 25:14-30, Jesus shares a parable about three men who were given talents (a denomination of money in Jesus' time). The parable compares the money to a talent, ability, or skill that you have been given and what you should do with your talents. What I love about this parable is that each of the three men was given at least one talent. And if they used their talent they were able to increase the number of talents they possessed. Only the man who did not put his talent to good use was stripped of his talent. Every woman, even you, has been given at least one talent; the key is to figure out what they are and how you can use them to honor God and advance his kingdom.

In the beginning of my Christian walk I felt inadequate in fulfilling God's plan. I wasted many years trying to figure out how I fit into God's kingdom. I knew I had talents; I just wasn't sure how they could be used to honor God. I was trying to fit myself into a Christian mold that was often uncomfortable and weird to me. I did things because that was what Christians did. Don't get me wrong, I believed in the goal and what the purpose was for what

I was doing. The method just wasn't my style, and so I was awkward at many things, at best.

I was awkward at sharing my faith (even though I really wanted people to love God, too). I was awkward and crazy when I invited people into my home (although I loved having them there). I hate housework and I am not fond of everyday cooking. So having people over is always crazy for me. I do it because I love people and sharing my life with them, but it is not my talent.

So what am I good at? What are my passions? I feel very confident in front of a group. I enjoy public speaking and motivational teaching. I excel at building trust and rapport with my students and clients quickly. I love writing. I am especially talented in business writing. I desire to help people achieve their best, especially women. I love being around women and just hanging out with them. I am good at planning things. And I am relatively good with fashion (really personal presence) and helping women create their look and style so they feel comfortable and gorgeous all at the same time.

What does all this mean for you? It means you start taking an inventory of what you love to do, what you are good at, and what others regularly compliment you on. Then figure out how you can put those talents and passions into service in your home, church, workplace, and community. You will find your Christian walk much more enjoyable as God intended if you put your efforts into serving God and others in ways you love and are passionate about.

Your first role as a *Divine Princess* is to love and obey God with all your heart, soul, and mind; then to share that love with others (Matt. 22:36-40). God wants you to use the talents he has given you to fulfill his purpose in your life. Here are some examples of how to use your talents to honor God:

- If you are a good cook, invite people into your home for a meal, cook for the church picnic, or bring a meal to a sick church member or friend.
- If you love children, serve in your youth ministry or organize a youth function.
- If you possess patience and compassion, visit the sick and elderly or be part of the grief recovery ministry.
- If you love technology and computer design, offer to oversee the church's website, create flyers, or print invitations to church. You could even offer your services to the public as a way of meeting people to share the Word with.

No matter what your talent or passion, use it to serve the Lord and to reach out to others in a natural and sincere way. Your passion will affect people in a way that causes them to ask what is different about you. You will naturally create opportunities to share your faith and help others to love Jesus.

Believe and Do Not Doubt

> For nothing is impossible with God.
>
> (Luke 1:37)

This Scripture, my favorite in the entire Bible, describes the story of Mary receiving the news from the angel Gabriel that God would cause her to conceive a child even though she was not married. Mary's response was that of a humble servant. Do you remember her response to Gabriel?

> I am the Lord's servant, Mary answered. May it be to me as you have said.
>
> (Luke 1:38)

Mary's faith was acknowledged and blessed by God.

> Blessed is she who has believed that what the Lord has said to her will be accomplished!
>
> (Luke 1:45)

Just like Mary, you can believe the Lord and not doubt. This can be hard, especially if you are like me—naturally skeptical, inquisitive, and possess an analytical mind, which usually demands proof of whatever anyone says.

Although there may be times when maintaining trust in God is hard, it can be done with consistent prayer and focus. Doubt causes confusion, frustration, guilt, and shame, and often leads to sin. The Bible is your foundation for building the kind of faith Mary possessed. Prayer must be part of your daily life. It is in prayer that you will find peace to follow God's commands. Staying focused requires self-control, a characteristic of God, which you did inherit from the Lord.

> For God did not give [you] a spirit of timidity, but a spirit of power, of love and of self-discipline.
>
> (2 Tim. 1:7)

Never Give Up

Your Christian walk is a journey. The Bible refers to it as a race (2 Tim. 4:7); a race that is won only by those who persevere and never give up. I have had times in my life when I wanted to walk away from God. I wanted to stop going to church because I was tired of going every week, and attending all the church functions. I wanted to stop giving contributions to the church because I wanted to spend my money—*really God's money*—on something else.

Fortunately, those moments have been brief. Yet, I *have* thought about walking away. I am a realist in some ways, and as I mature in my spirituality, I know I am not above falling away from God. I am weak without the Lord, and when I decide not to trust in him, I might do anything. Certainly, I am capable of all kinds of evil without God in my life as evidenced by my past.

For you, it is necessary to find those things or people that will help anchor you, especially in times of hardship and suffering. Memorize Scriptures that bring you peace and assure you of God's love, power, and devotion to your well being. Know which friends (*SWOFs*) you can go to who will listen with love and patience, provide a safe place for you to share openly, and guide you with Scriptures and not just their opinion. And commit yourself to running the race marked out for you until you reach the finish line…heaven (Phil. 3:14).

Don't waist any more time. Consider this chapter and the last as a spiritual checklist to cultivate and maintain a relationship with the heavenly Father. Do not approach it with disdain and automation, but with eagerness and hope. God will know your heart.

Do what is necessary to begin a true relationship with God or strengthen the relationship you have. So what do you need to do now? Study out a principle of God to overcome a current struggle? Share with a friend to receive wise and spiritual counsel? Or do you have to discover your talents so you can put them to use? Do it now! As the old cliché says, "There is no time like the present." Remember this moment in time is a gift from God. That's why it's called *the present*. Use it wisely.

Whatever your next step, remember to pray for God to make it clear to you what specifically you need to do. I believe your heart is intricately intertwined with God and in your subconscious you are drawn to the Lord. The joy of the Lord is waiting for you; all you have to do is embrace him and his purpose for your life.

Deepen Your Personal Convictions

Read: James 1:2-8; Matthew 21:21-22; Matthew 25:14-30

1. What are two things you are doing currently to be reconciled to Christ?

2. What are three talents you have and how can you use those talents to serve God and others?

3. What challenge do you foresee in using your talents for God?

4. What fruit will be produced when you use your talents for God?

5. Pray daily to believe in your ability to serve God well. Pray to find new and encouraging ways to use your talents to serve God and others.

CHAPTER 12

Ambassador of Love

We are therefore Christ's ambassadors, as though God were making his appeal through us. We implore you on Christ's behalf: Be reconciled to God. God made him who had no sin to be sin for us, so that in him we might become the righteousness of God.

(2 Cor. 5:20-21)

Living as a *Divine Princess* is a huge responsibility, yet one for which you are well equipped. Remember the Lord has given you everything you need to be successful, happy, fulfilled, and effective.

While writing this chapter I visited one of my sister churches in West Los Angeles. The minister's message was about living your heart's desire. I felt like God was speaking directly to me. I had been trying to close out this book with a message that would inspire you, give you knowledge, and provide you with practical things you could do right away. I want you to be crystal clear about how to live *divinely*.

I am certain you will understand every good thing you have in Christ when you:

1. Get right with God and stay right with God;
2. Fulfill your God-given mission of sharing Christ with others; and
3. Discover the specific talents God has given you and get to using them to honor the Lord in your unique and passionate way.

As a *Divine Princess* you truly embrace your *divinity* by realizing your place in the family of God, tapping into the power of a relationship with Christ, and honoring the Lord with your talents and passions by doing what you love to do. Your service to the Lord is your way of loving God and expressing your gratefulness for Christ's sacrifice for your life.

The Bible calls you to be an ambassador for Christ. He is making his appeal to others through you (2 Cor. 5:20). Your role as a *Divine Princess* is to represent God in all you do. You're like the secretary of state or the ambassador to a foreign nation; through your talents and godly pursuits you can honor the Lord in ways that make your light shine, so the message of God is spread throughout the world.

The message of God is love…simple, pure, unconditional, eternal, majestic love; one four letter word that holds immeasurable power. Love is the very thing each and every woman longs for. Even Scripture states a man must love his wife (Eph. 5:25, 33).

> My command is this: Love each other as I have loved you. Greater love has no one than this, that he lay down his life for his friends.
>
> (John 15:12-13)

That is exactly what Jesus did for you. He laid down his life so you might live.

You are the hope of the Lord. God sent Jesus with a message of love that includes forgiveness, grace, mercy, salvation, and eternal life. No greater message has one ever heard than the message of Jesus.

When Jesus ascended to heaven, he left you with the Great Commission to take care of his sheep: love them, teach them, and show them the way.

> God has given us the task of telling everyone what he is doing. God uses us to persuade men and women to drop their differences and enter into God's work of making things right between them. We are speaking for Christ himself now: Become friends with God; he's already a friend with you.
>
> (2 Cor. 5:19-21, THE MESSAGE)

Your righteous life and the use of your talents will persuade men and women to follow God. You have been appointed as an Ambassador of Love. An ambassador is appointed by the head of the nation. God is the head of our nation; there is no higher entity than the Creator of the Universe. Like any good father, God has a plan. He created you to become his righteousness on earth. He created you to be his Ambassador of Love. Like any official government appointed ambassador, you must have a clear understanding of the message you represent. In order to go and perform your godly mission you must reconcile yourself to God. You must take your place in God's family as a daughter, embracing your *divinity*. Once you have been reconciled to the Father, you will have full authority to go and share the message of the Lord persuading men and women to follow him.

Queen Esther was an Ambassador of Love. When faced with a challenging and life-threatening situation, she did not shrink back in fear. She turned to the Lord for courage and strength through fasting and prayer. She put her life on the line and her actions and faith saved millions of people. She was blessed because she portrayed the heart of Jesus. You can be like Queen Esther: a patient, faithful, selfless, and courageous leader—an Ambassador, leading the way to help others find eternal salvation, hope, and love.

Imagine you have been invited to a wonderful banquet in honor of Christ Jesus. You are there to represent the Lord in his absence. He will be attending the banquet, but he has been delayed. He has sent you ahead to prepare a way for him. He has sent you because he knows you can represent him well. Jesus knows and trusts your heart and integrity to present his message to the host of the banquet and the guests. You arrive at the banquet hall in a sparkling, jewel-encrusted, 24K, horse-drawn carriage ready to fulfill your mission. The footman helps you out of the carriage, bowing as you let go of his hand. You look up and there is a magnificent palace, surrounded by lush, colorful landscaping like that in a painting by Monet. You can smell the sweet aroma of fresh cut roses, azaleas, and eucalyptus trees. Your eyes are overwhelmed by the perfect blend of vibrant colors in all shades of purple, red, orange, yellow, and green. You take each stair as if floating on air. As you approach the tall, heavy French doors they open as if by magic. The trumpets begin to sound. The crowded room becomes quiet and still; all eyes are on you as you step forward in the most beautiful embroidered, white silk gown you have ever seen. A brilliant light is emanating powerfully from your essence. In a clear, majestic, and commanding voice your name is announced… *(insert your whole name)*, Ambassador of Love for Christ Jesus, Savior, and Son of God. You enter the room and many guests flee from you, fighting their demons and questioning themselves with each step. But a few guests are drawn to your light with inquisitive eyes and an open heart. They want to know what sets you apart; why peace befell them the moment you entered the room. In your right hand you hold a scroll with the life-changing message of Jesus. Each letter dipped in gold as a sign of importance and urgency. Hope, compassion, faith, and the love of Jesus are held in your heart to share with all who will listen. You greet your hosts and fellow Ambassadors. Then you embrace the opportunity the Lord has placed before you and begin to share the story of how God's love has changed your life forever.

Yes, the vision of a fairytale (this *is* a story about being a princess). And yes, real life is not quite as perfect and glamorous as the depiction of a golden carriage, trumpets, a gown, and a scroll dipped in gold; but the message of Jesus is no less important. You are still called to be an Ambassador of Love even in rags, poverty, a noisy, crime-infested backdrop, a hesitant audience of one, and only your memory of the Scriptures to guide you.

The purpose for your life is to share the Word of God with others. And until you embrace this mission you will wander through life and question what you missed. You will wonder if your current, simple existence is all there is to life. Don't wait until you are standing before God answering for your powerless life to realize God has more in store for you than just carpools and grocery shopping, folding laundry and cooking dinner, corporate reports and boring meetings, blogging and text messaging, and liposuction and breast implants. God has a very real, opulent, and majestic purpose for Y-O-U!

The Lord *knows* that through the magnificent and vibrant use of your talents you will be able to reach your brothers and sisters that need to return to the Father's house to be filled with love, grace, mercy, peace, and hope. Regardless of your circumstances, the simplicity of your surroundings, or the condition of the hearts around you, your mission must be completed. If you pursue Jesus, you will be armed with the Word of Truth, faith, confidence, wisdom, and the invincible message of love. So no matter what your gift is, may you do it with eagerness and compassion for others.

> We have different gifts, according to the grace given us. If a [wo]man's gift is prophesying, let (her) use it in proportion to [her] faith. If it is serving, let [her] serve; if it is teaching let [her] teach; if it is encouraging, let [her] encourage; if it is contributing to the needs of others, let [her] give generously; if it is leadership, let [her] govern diligently; if it is showing mercy, let [her] do it cheerfully.
>
> (Rom. 12:6-8)

In order to recognize your talents you have to honestly assess your skills, not hindered by low self-esteem or negative self talk. You are valuable because God loves you and he paid the ultimate sacrifice for you. Understanding your self-worth according to God and not the world, empowers you to do the work of the Lord with passion, joy, peace, devotion, and consistency for a lifetime. Marianne Williamson wrote a poem called "Our Greatest Fear." The poem is amazing. It encourages you to always let your light shine because in doing so you give others permission to shine, too. You are powerful beyond measure because you have God washing you off, lifting you up, and making you strong.

So remember who you are...woman...the masterpiece of the creation of the universe. Created by the best designer this world will or has ever seen. You are the magnum opus of the Lord. You are unique, a one-of-a-kind creation. No one in all the history of the earth is exactly like you. You are loved more than any other creation of God's. You are smart, talented, and majestic because you were made in his *divine* image. The Lord basks in the brilliance of your beauty. Your value is far beyond rubies, diamonds, gold or silver. You shine brighter than any star in the sky. You bring him immeasurable joy. *Every* moment of *every day* the Creator of the Universe desires to be with you.

Go and let your light shine to manifest the glory of God in your life. Go and reach out to others using your unique talents and deep passions. Love the Father the way he has loved you, with everything he has, sacrificing that which was most precious to him and giving it to you as a reminder of his eternal and masterful love.

You are empowered to be the amazing and talented daughter of The King...spiritual royalty. You belong to the Lord, so embrace your divinity. Go as Christ's Ambassador, bringing God's message of love to others as his...*Divine Princess, fearfully and wonderfully made.*

Deepen Your Personal Convictions

Read: Isaiah 6:8; 1 John 1:5-7; 2 Corinthians 5:16-21

1. Like Isaiah, will you respond to God's call for you?

2. What two things are you doing to mature and grow your faith so you can represent God well?

3. List two people you will share the Word with in the next seven days. Or list who you will seek guidance from within the next seven days about the purpose God has for you.

4. List two people you can serve within the next seven days. How will you serve them?

5. Pray daily to embrace your purpose as Christ's Ambassador of Love.

Closing Prayer

Dear Father,

Your supreme wisdom and love has guided me through the journey of writing this book. I have enjoyed every minute of it, even the times of remembering painful events, because they remind me of my need for you. I felt my own heart being discipled and I was convicted by your powerful Word again and again. Please help my Sister to take this message and act on it like the Woman Who Bled and the Sinful Woman. Please let her be like Queen Esther, relying on you for courage; strength; an open door; a gentle, yet powerful voice; and salvation. Please help her to take her place in your family and to embrace her *divinity* as a daughter of The King. Create in her a desire to pursue your principles and use her God-given talents in ways that glorify and honor you, serve others, and spread your magnificent love.

Thank you for allowing me to be an Ambassador of Love. Allow my faith to grow and mature and become all you desire it to be. I pray you place more messages of your Word and your desires on my heart to share with your daughters. Please let the light of this book shine around the globe, bringing peace and hope and love to every woman in need and every woman seeking you.

I feel honored to have been chosen to share such an encouraging and timely message as *Woman: Wonderfully Made*. Thank you for the many blessings you have bestowed upon me. Please keep me centered and focused on you. Please help me to be a great steward of all you have given me. Please bless your daughter who has read this book; spur her to action in maturing her relationship with you and in sharing her faith with others.

To you, my Father, Lord, and Savior be the glory, forever and ever,

Amen

Divine is the Princess

Called to be the Daughter of the King,
Divine is the Princess she.

Forgiveness is the jewel encrusted crown,
away from her no one can take.
Grace is the royal robe of Love,
cleansed pure the scars of her past.
Bestowed with the holy scepter of Salvation,
marked out for her the race she runs.

Merciful is the hand of God,
from the enemy she is protected.
Gifted with divine Wisdom,
carefully placed is her every step.
Refreshed by the Word of Truth,
deep inside her soul immersed.

Humility held within her heart,
dripping from each spoken word.

Passion fuels Majestic Talents,
by deliberate thought actions are spurred.
Victorious in the Mission of saints,
sought and saved are the lost.
Sacrificial in every way,
await in Heaven her treasures lie.
Inspired by the Love of Jesus,
honored with her life He is first.

Websites and Email Addresses

The following websites may provide additional information helpful to developing your faith and character. Views expressed in the websites and blogs may not represent Ayesha Glover, Pleasant Word Publishing, or Wine Press Publishing. In addition, website addresses and the information on the following websites may change after the publication of this book.

Directly email the author, Ayesha Glover, at **ayeshaglover@divineprincess.com.** Ayesha Glover is available for speaking engagements, spiritual training workshops for women, book club meetings, and book signings. Please contact the author with comments about the book and how God is changing your life.

Visit the *Divine Princess* website at **www.divineprincess.com.** *Divine Princess* is community for Christian women seeking a deeper relationship with God, inner spiritual beauty, fellowship, and fun. You will find a discount coupon for merchandise at the end of the book. *Divine Princess* also has logo wear. Go to the website to purchase *Woman: Wonderfully Made* logo wear, and other items.

Visit Ayesha Glover's blog at **http://ayeshaglover.authorweblog.com.** The author posts to her blog a couple of times per week.

Visit the Greater Las Vegas Church of Christ at **www.glvcc.org.** GLVCC is a non-denominational Christian church that earnestly preaches, teaches, and lives by the Bible. If you live in the Las Vegas area or you will be visiting Las Vegas, you are welcome to come and worship with Ayesha Glover and her spiritual family.

Visit Disciples Today at **www.disciplestoday.org.** Disciples Today is the current website for the (former) "International Churches of Christ" to share national and international information with members and interested individuals all over the world. Visit this site to find a church near you.

Visit BibleGateway.com at **www.biblegateway.com.** BibleGateway is a free online tool for studying the Bible. It provides the Bible in different Biblical translations, as well as different languages.

Visit Pleasant Word Christian Publishing at **www.pleasantword.com.** Pleasant Word is a division of Wine Press Publishing, a traditional Christian publishing house. Pleasant Word offers opportunities to self-publish your original work.

Divine Princess Merchandise

To purchase *Divine Princess* merchandise at a discount, use the coupon code below. Visit our website at: **www.divineprincess.com**.

LaVergne, TN USA
04 March 2010
174903LV00001B/1/P